CAMBODIA: LAND OF CONTRASTS

Also by Ruth Tooze

AMERICA

SILVER FROM THE SEA

OUR RICE VILLAGE IN CAMBODIA

NIKKOS AND THE PINK PELICAN

CAMBODIA:
LAND OF
CONTRASTS

BY RUTH TOOZE

illustrated with photographs

THE VIKING PRESS · NEW YORK

*To my Cambodian friends, especially those
in the Ministry of Education,
and to the fellow Americans who,
because of our work there together,
share an interest in this country of Southeast Asia*

ACKNOWLEDGMENTS

Most of the pictures in this book were taken by Dr. Thomas S. Weir of the United States Administration for International Development. Many were taken by Sandy McCaw and by the author during the time when all three of us were working in Cambodia with the same government agency. The author is very grateful to these friends for the use of their pictures, and to the French Embassy Press and Information division for the use of the photographs on pages 2, 3, 37, 38, 42, 48, 80, 81, 95, 97, 110, 111, 136.

CONTENTS

ILLUSTRATIONS

CAMBODIA: LAND OF CONTRASTS

CAMBODIA

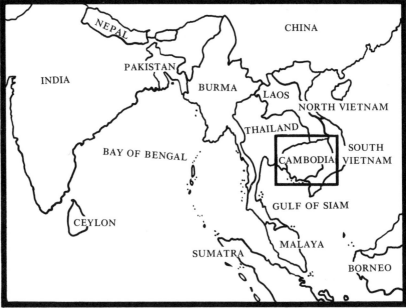

1

CAMBODIA,
A RICE-GROWING LAND

Cambodia is a small country — about the size of the state of Missouri — situated in the heart of the Southeast Asian peninsula. Although Cambodia, along with Laos and Vietnam, was for about one hundred years part of a protectorate known as French Indochina, it is neither Indian nor Chinese. It is a distinct country. Its people have unique characteristics, and its language has no relation to that of any of its neighbors. The nature of the land has helped to determine the nature and habits of the people who live in this hot section of the tropics.

Cambodia is a land of great contrasts. Its central region, a wide basin lying almost at sea level, is surrounded by mountains. Its weather changes sharply from a bleak, dry season to a steaming moist season. And its days begin with pale red sunrises and end with gorgeous coppery sunsets. Oxcarts on the roads haul produce to market while jets fly overhead to land at a modern airport. In Phnom Penh, the capital city, unpaved packed mud streets, with gutters on either side full of waste and rubbish, meander alongside a modern paved street with traffic lights. In the same city, a royal palace stands among thousands of *paillottes*, one- or two-room wooden houses on stilts. Wooden plows exactly like those used centuries ago turn the

The mighty Mekong

soil in fields bordering roads where automobiles speed by. Old men dressed as their ancestors dressed mingle with young men in modern Western clothes. Village orchestras of handmade drums and flutes and marimbas share popularity with modern "combos" of Western wind and percussion instruments.

The life blood of Cambodia is the mighty Mekong River, fourth longest river in the world, which rises far up in the snow-covered mountains of China and flows down through south China, Laos, Cambodia, and Vietnam to the sea, where it fans out into a great delta not unlike that of the Mississippi. Like the Amazon, the Nile, and the great Yellow River of China, it brings life to the country through which it flows. During the long winter, while the northern mountains are frozen and snow-covered, no water flows, and the fields of the southern lands lie sere and dry. There is little water in pools and streams. The river's water level is so low that its banks rise like high bluffs on either side. The sun shines mercilessly down from a cloudless sky for about six months, from October through April. During this time there is nothing to do in the fields. There is little fishing in the low waters. Many people are idle.

Then, in May, cloud masses begin to form and move majestically across the sky, like great white mountains with shadows of gray and purple. The children love these clouds, so full of shapes like dragons and giants, wild animals and flying birds, chariots and airplanes. They look and look, and the older children tell stories about these cloud characters to the younger ones.

At first the clouds roll in and roll away, leaving not a drop of rain. But gradually, as the days go by, the white cloud mountains begin to appear almost every day soon after the noon hour. They darken to gray, to blue, to purple, ominously shadowing the world below. Then the rain comes down, the long-awaited beneficent rain.

At the same time the snows in the high mountains to the north in China begin to melt and fill the rivers, which rush down in torrents into the Mekong. The rains in the country below add more water to the swollen river. It rises two feet, six feet, ten feet, twenty, thirty feet! The high banks disappear. A boat on the river floats level with the land along its edge. The river overflows its banks. Now there is much action along the river, for everyone washes himself as well as his clothes there, and drinks the water.

Now the rice farmers have much to do as the streams, pools, and rice fields fill with water. They come out from the villages along the river and plant seed beds of rice on land nearby. Soon the squares of close-packed rice shoots appear. They are green — a living bright green, luminous in the sunshine as if the light came from within rather than without. This rice green, this special bright light green, is as characteristic of young rice shoots as olive-green is of the leaves of an olive tree, or apple-green of the leaves of an apple tree.

A farmer plowing his rice field

By July the fields are standing in water. Around each field is a ditch like a moat. A farmer hitches his wooden plow to two water buffalo to turn the heavy mud and prepare the field for planting the seedlings. Back and forth, back and forth the length of his field, he clucks and calls to the slow-moving gray creatures as he and they slosh knee-deep through the mud and the water. Now and then birds come to rest on the spreading horns of the buffalo and take a little ride.

When the fields are plowed boys bring bunches of shoots from the seed beds near their homes and stack them together near the center of each field. The women come and stand knee-deep in the water,

16   CAMBODIA

with backs bent as they transplant each single shoot from the seed bed to the thick, soft mud of the field:

Pull a shoot, push it into the mud, pinch it firm.

Pull a shoot, push it into the mud, pinch it firm.

Row after row after row fills the flooded fields as the women plant the rice shoots hour after hour after hour. Pointed hats shield their heads from the hot sun, and black blouses protect their arms and shoulders. Their black trousers are pulled up and tucked tight above their knees. The women sweat and toil long hours under the burning sun, knee-deep in the water, planting their rice.

Narrow ditches surround each field. Soon boys with names like Seng and Tek and Mao appear, carrying long bamboo poles and bits of bait. They begin to fish in the water of the rice field. The fish bite quickly. They are not large, but there are many of them. So families get both rice and fish, staples of their diet, from the overflowing waters of the great river, the mighty Mekong, the giver of life to this land.

The fishing is fun, not work, for these boys. But the rice planting, plowing, and transplanting is hard work for many men and women, although it lasts for only a few days. Since there is no cultivating or

Women transplanting rice

weeding to do, there are many days of idle waiting for the grain to ripen. There are those who say a Cambodian rice farmer seldom works more than a hundred days in a year. During the rest of the time he watches and waits.

In December and January comes the harvest. The rice farmers use long, curved rice knives for harvesting. Each knife has a small sharp prong that cuts the rice on the forward swing and a large wooden curve that gathers a new bunch for cutting on the back swing. In the lowlands, the farmers carve the knife handles into the shape of the tail of a *humpsa*, a mythical bird said to bring good luck to lowland rice growers. In the highlands, the farmers carve their knife handles into the shapes of dragons, said to bring good luck to rice growers there. The oil and sweat from the farmers' hands stain and polish the handles to a rich dark brown.

When the rice stalks are cut, they are stacked in bunches for the rice to dry, and when it has dried, the heads are cut off. Then the women toss the whole rice grains in large, round woven bamboo trays, winnowing the kernels from the husks. Each family now has much of its reserve of food for the coming year. It is put in large clay jars or huge baskets of tightly woven rice straw. In addition some families have extra rice to sell.

Year after year this cycle of planting, transplanting, waiting, harvesting, winnowing the rice is repeated in many parts of this country, for rice is the chief product of the land.

Fishing
in the rice field

Playing in a field of growing rice

A lowland farmer's rice knife

Threshing

A rice village

Cambodia's farmers live in typical rice villages, most of them situated on or near the river. Each has its group of *paillottes,* houses
built of bamboo strips and palm leaves, standing high on stilts so as
to be above the water and mud in the rainy season. Each has a *wat*
(temple), usually Buddhist, with its group of saffron-robed *bonzes*
(priests and monks) and small wing-roofed buildings. Each has a
school of one to four rooms. And each has a market where farmers,
fishermen, and makers of baskets and pots bring their wares at dawn
every day. The farmers go out from their villages to work in the rice
fields nearby.

A *paillotte* usually has one or two rooms and is used for little but
sleeping. One climbs up to it on a rickety ladder or narrow shaky

Paillottes during the rainy season

steps. There are seldom any windows, but space is almost always left between the walls and the roof. Sometimes the walls go only halfway up. There may be a door for an entrance, or most of the front may be left open. The people sleep on woven rice-straw mats, sometimes on a bamboo platform raised a little above the floor.

The farmer's wife may have a few crude iron pots and cooking utensils, but she does the cooking outside of the house in a small fire hole dug nearby. Few Cambodians eat early in the day, so most children go off to school without breakfast and eat whenever they feel like it. The mother may cook a little rice and fish at home, but she and the children are just as likely to run down the road and buy a bit of rice and fish or a chunk of sugar cane to chew. A man or woman with long bamboo pole over the shoulder, small charcoal stoves balanced on one end, and baskets with a little food and a few dishes on the other, squats and sets up his "restaurant" anywhere

22   CAMBODIA

any time. It seems that one always sees someone eating. It is all very casual.

Most Cambodians are Buddhists. Buddha (the name means the Enlightened One) was born in India about six hundred years before Christ. A member of a Hindu family of wealth, he spent his early life shielded from most of the evils of the world: illness, poverty, and death. But as he grew into manhood, Buddha became aware of these evils and was not content to stay home. He went to remote places to meditate, pray, and seek a way of life that would make man truly happy. He thought profoundly about man's suffering and its causes. Ultimately he offered mankind an eight-point plan of discipline which he believed would lead to the cessation of suffering:

These are the eight points:
1. Right Belief
2. Right Aspiration or Resolve
3. Right Speech
4. Right Conduct or Action
5. Right Means of Livelihood
6. Right Endeavor or Effort
7. Right Memory or Reflection
8. Right Meditation

The first six are moral or ethical self-disciplines. The seventh is intellectual; the eighth, mystical.

Many people listened to this teaching and became known as Buddhists, or followers of Buddha. Their religion, called Buddhism, spread from India to China and Japan and much of Southeast Asia, including Cambodia.

So the little stucco *wat* with winged roof and inside room with statues of Buddha and often pictures depicting his life story is important to each Cambodian village as a center for all festivals and much social life. The offerings to the image of Buddha usually consist of flowers, fruits, and burning punk sticks. Nearly every Cambodian man is expected to give at least one year of his life as a *bonze*, and most of them do. Some boys become *bonzes* when they

A small wat

are only twelve years old, and a few remain *bonzes* all their lives. You can see both boys and men, ranging in age from twelve to sixty and older, in the saffron robes. Their heads are shaven, and, because the sun is so hot, each carries a large white umbrella. A *bonze* may not work or cook for himself, or eat after eleven o'clock in the morning. So from about nine to eleven o'clock each morning the *bonzes* stand in front of homes with empty urns to receive gifts of food. The food is usually rice, and many times only a little of that. As a result, the priests are all very thin. No wonder a common expression in Cambodia is "as shrunken as a *bonze*'s stomach."

There is often a school connected with the *wat*. Many boys become *bonzes* just in order to get an extra year or two of school. And always a *bonze* receives a certain amount of respect.

Nearly every village has a government school. Although attendance is not compulsory, the number of schools all over the country is increasing, for more and more parents want their children to go to school. The largest number of children, ages six to nine, is in the first grade. About one half of these go on to second grade; their

Bonzes coming to beg for food

numbers diminish as they go through the six grades of primary school. A very small number attends secondary school.

The typical Cambodian school is a small oblong structure built on the ground, usually of bamboo and palm. The floor is usually dirt. One of the side walls of palm leaves may be on horizontal hinges, so that it can be raised to let in air occasionally. The room is crowded with many small, narrow desks with narrow seats attached; each bench is long enough for four to six pupils. There are anywhere from fifty to ninety pupils in the classroom. The teacher has usually been through the six grades, though in an exceptional case he may have continued through secondary school (comparable with grades seven, eight, and nine in the United States). He has a table and a chair, a small blackboard and a little chalk, and an outline of the course of study from the country's Ministry of Education.

The little children with their thin bodies and large inquiring eyes walk each morning from their homes in the village and from nearby

Children in school (sixth grade)

smaller villages to stand with their teacher and sing their national anthem, called "*Nokoreach*," as one boy proudly raises the flag. They then march two by two into the dark, dusty, crowded rooms to sit on those narrow benches from seven to eleven o'clock every morning. They go home to spend the middle of the day out of the heat, return to school at two-thirty every afternoon, and stay until five-thirty.

In the lower grades the pupils listen to what the teacher tells them from his outline and then chant it back in unison. After the fourth grade, pupils have notebooks into which they copy what the teacher writes on the board. They learn the Cambodian alphabet and how to form its letters, numbers, a little arithmetic, and something about the health, manners, and geography of the Eastern world. In

A teacher and children in a government school near Phnom Penh

A village market

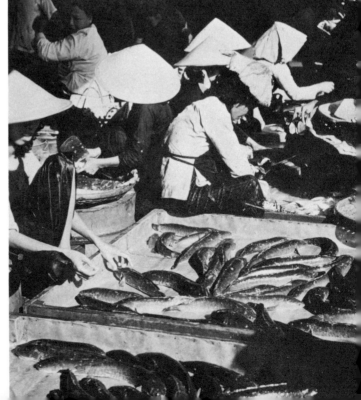

Fish for sale!

secondary schools some science and history may be added. All the teaching is in Cambodian, the Khmer language, during the first three grades. In the fourth grade the pupils begin to study French. The use of French continues because Cambodia was once part of French Indochina. By the sixth grade, some classes are conducted in French as well as in Cambodian. Beyond the sixth grade, all the teaching is in French.

But changes are in the making. With American aid, a teacher-training school has been opened where Cambodian young people are given four years of training in modern concepts of teaching, such as using books, developing projects, and making scientific experiments. In each of Cambodia's sixteen provinces, American aid has also built an experimental school out of more permanent material than bamboo and palm, and has helped improve a selected group of about one hundred primary schools. Each year more Cambodian children want to go to school.

The lively center of village life however, is not the school but the market — a large, open square. Long before the dawn people begin to come with rice, vegetables, fruits, fish, chickens, pigs, and many foods unknown to people of the Western world. Some carry most of their produce in large baskets balanced on their heads. Some have two-wheeled oxcarts to carry their goods. Some fill the stalls, others sit in their spaces of ground with their few baskets. Many a merchant (if such a grand title can be used for the seller of a very few pieces of sugar cane, or a few fish, or a couple of roasted sparrows, or fried tarantulas) sits on his haunches in his allotted space in the open area. The cloth-sellers usually stay under a crude wooden roof that covers some of the stalls and arrange their bolts of cloth to show off the colors, protected from the strong rays of the sun. By the time the sun appears at the horizon every inch of space is full.

Soon the whole village is at the market, which becomes very noisy as the buyers, who are usually women, bargain for the best possible prices. No one expects to get the price he asks. The seller, usually a man, starts too high; the buyer, too low. The seller comes down a

A restaurant on wheels

bit, and the buyer raises her offer a bit, until finally a satisfactory price is agreed upon. The process is expected and is actually enjoyed by both.

Meanwhile, food vendors have set up their tiny stoves or carts, and many people stop to buy some soup or rice or fish, eating casually, as always.

By ten o'clock very little food is left, and people are wending their way home, often with a small piece of pork, crab, or shrimp in one hand, and a cabbage or squash or mango or a small bunch of green bananas in the other. (Only a few of the thirty-five varieties of bananas in Cambodia have to become yellow to be ripe enough to eat.) A few things like shrimps or peas or bean sprouts will be wrapped in a neat little cornucopia made by the seller on the spot from a large palm or banana leaf and tied with a loop for carrying with a palm-leaf cord. But fish or chunks of meat are simply threaded on a cord and carried without wrapping. Flies and mosquitoes cover most of the food not only while it is in the market but on its way home as well.

For shelter from the sun, nearly every Cambodian adult has a dark red or brownish checked scarf about half a yard wide and a half to two yards long. This is draped loosely around the head, with the end flipped over casually. The same scarf is used to tie a baby to his mother's back, to make a base for a heavy pot to be carried on the head, to wipe used dishes or the brow, or to polish fruit for sale. It is a very useful possession.

In the larger villages, there is in addition to the market a short main street or square with shops selling hardware, rope and rope products, bicycles, jewelry, and cloth. Most larger villages also have one or two restaurants that would be recognized as such by a Westerner. But in Cambodia a restaurant may be anything from a squatting seller with a tiny stove and a few dishes, to a little stand on wheels, to a room with eight or ten tables and a cook. The really well set-up shops, however, are nearly always owned by Chinese, for the Chinese control most of the business in Cambodia as they do in all the countries of Southeast Asia. They are quicker than most Cambodians, and sharper in business, but they have to pay heavier taxes to the government than do the Cambodians.

The people in every village are a friendly group, and much of their work is done cooperatively. Since the houses are all open, there is no such thing as privacy, either personal or family. Except for

A Cambodian family

sleeping, everything is done in public: eating, washing clothes in whatever water is near, bathing in the same spot, talking, sitting, watching. Once in a while after the sun has set, a boy brings out his drum, especially if the moon is shining, and the young people join him in singing the folk songs they all know and love, and dancing the graceful *lamthon*, the typical Cambodian dance. The melodies are traditional. Words for them are often made up spontaneously — about the people themselves, a recent event, or a current interest. Soon the adults join in the fun while the younger children sit back

The family of a silversmith in Kompong Luong

in a circle, looking and watching, looking and watching. Everyone shares in the life of the village in Cambodia. Children are with their parents as they work, or play, or sit and talk. Always the families are together.

2

CAMBODIA,
LAND OF THE KHMERS

Although Cambodia is a small country today, it once ruled the entire Southeast Asian peninsula. One still sees in the people and in their ways of living an awareness of this ancient heritage of greatness. Cambodians have pride in their language; pride in their music, dancing, and visual arts; pride in their country, the land of the Khmers; and pride in being Cambodian.

The origins of Cambodia and the sources of its pride are hinted at in legends and folk tales. Facts are woven into its legends; and its legends are often taught as facts. According to the legends, Indian civilization in Cambodia had two sources: the mountain men, said to be descendants of the divine bird, the Garuda; and the lowlands river men, descendants of the divine fish or serpent, the Naga. These symbols — the Garuda bird and the Naga or snake — are preserved in ancient temples and carvings as well as in modern ones.

The recorded history of Cambodia begins about the first century A.D. with a period known as Funan or Founan. At this time three distinct peoples lived in the lower Mekong area: the Funanese, of Chinese origin; the Chams, of Malay origin; and the Khmers, whose origins are unknown. By the third century the Funanese were in complete control, but then an Indian Brahman gained power.

During the next two centuries, the various peoples of Cambodia were completely Indianized. The Cambodian king became identified with the Indian deities of Vishnu and Siva, and he was worshiped as a god. The Indian legal code was introduced. Today, after fifteen hundred years, these Indian influences are still evident in the Cambodian concepts of law and law enforcement.

During the middle of the sixth century the chief vassal state to the south of Funan, Chen-La, where the Khmers lived, gained control over Funan and extended its empire to the borders of present-day China. This period lasted about two hundred and fifty years and was marked by continuous strife among many petty states, especially between the mountain men to the north and the river men to the south.

The name Cambodia derives from this time. The founder of the Khmer dynasty, according to legend, was Kambu Svayambhuva. So the sons of Kambu came to be known as Kambuja — in French, Cambodge; in English, Cambodia.

For many years the sons of Kambu moved their capital from city to city across the central plain of the Mekong delta. Then came their time of greatness, the years from 802 to 1432 A.D., known as the Angkor period. During this time the great city-temple, Angkor Thom, which became the capital, and the great mortuary temple, Angkor Wat, were built.

The Cambodian kings of this era, from Jayavarman II to Jayavarman VII, spread their power by sweeping conquests of most of Southeast Asia. Their empire included what is Laos today and even much of present-day Thailand. Some say that the Khmer kings exacted tribute from places as remote as Malaya and the Indonesian islands.

Today the Khmer temples constitute one of the world's largest historical remains. Over five hundred buildings, some still in ruins, some restored, are scattered over an area of many square miles. Gigantic masses of gray stone rise from the mighty jungle like multi-volume books of history, a record and a symbol of the magnificent Khmer civilization at the peak of its power. The giant towers and

The ruins at Angkor Thom

turrets connected with long corridors and walled enclosures once housed temples, shrines, halls of meditation, hospitals, libraries, and pavilions where the temple and palace dancers performed. Visiting them, one is reminded of the rise and fall of such other great civilizations as those of the Incas, the Mayas, the Egyptians, and the Greeks.

As the kingdom grew and prospered during the Angkor period, the city of Angkor Thom grew with it. Its many inhabitants built beautiful sandstone temples to their gods, which in the early part of the Angkor period were Hindu ones, Siva, Vishnu, and Brahma. All the temples in Angkor Thom show strong Indian influence. The four faces of the Buddha look forth from lofty towers, the symbol of his saving eye looking out over the world. The Hindu god, Vishnu, and other gods are carved in a thousand forms. Some of the vast

36   CAMBODIA

Towers of the Bayon at Angkor Thom

panoramas of detailed bas-reliefs on the walls tell the story of the
great Indian epic, the Adventure of Rama; others present climactic
scenes from the Hindu mythology which was so essential to Cambodian religion of the early Angkor period and traces of which are
still evident in the nation's arts today.

Although there were slaves in the kingdom, social welfare was a
genuine concern of the kings. Hospitals, rest homes, schools, and
even libraries were founded throughout the land. The arts also
flourished. But possibly the most notable achievement of this time
was the construction of the mortuary temple called Angkor Wat.
Angkor Wat was built on a site a short distance outside the city of
Angkor Thom by Suryavarman II, around the year 1130. At about
the same time this beautiful monument was being built to glorify
the Hindu gods, the newer religion from India, Buddhism, was on

CAMBODIA, LAND OF THE KHMERS   37

its way to Cambodia. And as more and more Cambodians became Buddhists, they turned their attention increasingly to peaceful activities.

About seventy years after Angkor Wat was built, the last strong Cambodian King, Jayavarman VII, led his people in the paths of peace as a devout Buddhist. He added many temples, walls, and portals with strong Buddhist influence to Angkor Thom. These helped make the city, with its decorations combining Hindu and Buddhist motifs, one of the most beautiful cities of the world. No doubt the Khmers were notable for more than their genius at building, but because the chief remnants of their magnificent civilization are architectural ruins, we naturally consider the building of Angkor Wat, Angkor Thom, and the nearby temples, to be their most spectacular achievement.

A charging army, depicted on the long wall of the gallery of Angkor Wat

One of the most interesting things about Angkor Thom is the Bayon, its largest temple, which some consider the most wonderful of all the Khmer monuments. It is made up of many shrines built around numerous courtyards and lies in the exact center of the ancient city. In court after court after court, there are lofty turrets and walled enclosures, elaborately decorated. On each of the four sides of the towers of its shrines appears a face of the compassionate Buddha. One long wall depicts in magnificent bas-relief the whole life of the time: the birth of a baby; the preparation of a meal; the preparations for a wedding; boats at sea with some men diving from them, some fishing; hosts of armies charging in battle, some on foot, some on mighty elephants. The humanist feeling introduced into religion by Buddhism expresses itself in these pictures of daily living.

Angkor Wat is also a masterpiece. The temple space occupies an area three-fifths of a mile square and is surrounded by a moat 650 feet wide. A paved causeway is the only approach to the temple. It leads from the surrounding country to a bridge which crosses the moat and which once brought worshipers into the temple itself.

The bas-reliefs of the temple present a panorama of 18,000 carved scenes depicting Hindu mythology and Khmer life. Walking up the long, wide main approach between balustrades, you see on either side magnificently carved Naga heads. Climbing the steep steps to the central high tower you look out over buildings, courtyards, and the surrounding countryside. Walking through the long majestic corridors you see walls on every inch of which are carved delicate traceries of leaves and flowers, gods, demons, elephants, monkeys, birds, snakes, and *apsaras*, or dancing maidens. How the Cambodians must have loved those *apsaras*, there are so many of them as statues, on cornices, in bas-relief on the walls!

Nearby are Preah Khan, Neak Pean, and many smaller temples featuring the four faces of the Indian god Siva, more gods and demons, more charming *apsaras*, more animals and birds, and details of everyday living. There are giant, majestic Naga heads on pillars and posts. On an elephant terrace, two long rows of carved

Approach to Angkor

The steep steps up to the central tower at Angkor Wat

A group of apsaras

elephants standing facing each other, imply the Cambodians' de-
pendence on the strength of these great jungle beasts. A statue of a
leper king stands in lonely splendor.

*Bas relief of apsaras
at Angkor Wat*

*Banteay Srei,
the women's temple*

Srei is the Cambodian word for women. A little distance to the northeast of Angkor Thom stands Banteay Srei, which means women's temple. Its carving is probably the most beautiful of that in any of the temples. Was it called Banteay Srei because it was carved by women, because it was built especially for priestesses, or because it was so small? One does not need to know the answer in order to enjoy its exquisite beauty.

To climb, to walk, to explore, to examine the ruins; to enjoy all the detailed beauty in the carving, all the grandeur of the complicated buildings, with their magnificent courtyards, corridors, long, walled enclosures, turrets, and towers surrounded by wide moats, start the wheels of conjecture and imagination turning. It is not difficult to visualize these vast courtyards crowded for a religious ceremony. You can almost see the king at the head of a great procession, riding one of a herd of two hundred thousand elephants. Golden parasols are held above him; there are elaborately embroidered garments and decorations both on him and on his elephant. Courtiers, priests, and attendants follow, also mounted on elephants. Then come the dancing girls, the jugglers, and the acrobats. All this grandeur moves slowly through throngs of people gathered for worship, sacrifice, and pleasure. (One inscription on a temple says that eighty thousand people were attached to one of the smaller temples alone!)

What happened to all this magnificence? For one thing, as Buddhism developed in Cambodia it not only was peace-loving but also de-emphasized large temples. For another, the Khmer kings' struggles against invading Thais, Chams, and Annamese used up the nation's strength and resources. The people were exhausted by all the great construction projects as well as by wars. Leadership diminished in quality. It takes only two or three weak kings in succession to permit the whole cultural pattern of a country to change. We observe this over and over in history.

After the death of Jayavarman VII about 1218 A.D., the Cambodian empire began to fall apart. Political as well as artistic energy

The jungle taking over a temple at Angkor Thom

declined. Thai influence increased; the Thais captured Angkor in 1353. The Kambujans recaptured it, only to lose it again to them. The Khmers gave up Angkor Thom as their capital. And the neglected city fell into a state of decline and ultimately of decadence as conquering neighbors looted and carried off its treasures.

Meanwhile, Buddhism made increasing inroads on Hinduism.

Without leaders to plan for them and force them to work, and with a decline of interest in the old gods and uncertainty about the new ones, the gentle, conquered Cambodians spent most of their strength and skill simply struggling to exist. And finally the jungle took over, slowly invading the magnificent temples and the majesty of Angkor — chiefly by the growth of one jungle tree, the bombex.

Bombex trees are tall and straight and slender. There are hundreds and hundreds of them in this part of the world. The bark is a creamy beige with dents in it like thumbprints on glass — breathtakingly beautiful as the brilliant tropical sunlight makes the satiny bark glow and nearby trees send lavender shadows dancing across its shining surface. Some twenty-five to forty feet above the ground, great flanges begin to grow from the trunk. From these, long curling roots wedge their way between the stones of buildings, curling around them until they are loosened and dislodged, and fall to the ground. The roots scarcely look like roots, since they are the same color as the tree; the giant snakelike coils look more animal than vegetable. It takes the bombex tree only one hundred or two hundred years to cause the complete destruction of a temple.

Other rapidly growing trees also cover the stones with a network of tangled small roots and pull them loose until they tumble. So the majestic temples built by powerful kings with vision and love of beauty have gradually disintegrated into jumbled heaps of rocks. We marvel at the buildings and wonder how the huge stones were carried from quarries and put in high places without the help of any machinery. We wonder how such an amazingly beautiful portrayal of life could have been carved in such detail in stone. We see the destruction and devastation caused by years of abandonment and neglect. And we see how the jungle took over.

Wind and water have worn away the sharp edges of many carvings in the soft sandstone. The mineral deposits from water, mosses, lichens, and other plant growth have tinted the rocks in a thousand shades of green, lavender, purple, apricot, and russet, with gray and black shadings. So, in a sense, the natural beauty of today rivals the man-made beauty and grandeur of yesterday.

Probably no one would ever have seen any of these buildings in their original grandeur if in 1876 the French archaeologist Henri Mouhot had not come upon the ruins of the great Angkor complex. Since then funds from France and other nations have made possible the slow reconstruction and restoration of many of the temples from the ruins he discovered. If one marvels at the manpower it took originally to design and build and carve Angkor Wat and Angkor Thom, one marvels almost equally at the skill involved in separating and numbering thousands upon thousands of stones and putting them back together as once they were. Edges are worn, corners are broken, but an amazing job of restoration has been done already and is still being carried on.

No wonder the modern Khmer is proud of the blood that flows in his veins. Today's Cambodians retain the grace of their forebears, so that you see the tableaux depicted in those stone tapestries come alive in the people. You see them especially when, once a year, the dancers from the royal palace perform in the great open space in front of Angkor Wat. As you watch them, it seems as if the *apsaras* on the wall have quickened to life and stepped out of their stone existence to delight an audience once more. The sons of Kambu, the Cambodians, survive — a gentle, proud people, whose deep cultural roots give them strength to attack the difficult problems of growing into a modern nation and making a place in the industrialized and scientific world of today.

The struggle between the Thais and Khmers went on even after 1430, when the Khmers were finally conquered, until 1864, when Cambodia became a French protectorate. By 1887 Cambodia was part of an Indochinese Union (Cambodia, Vietnam, and Laos) under a special French lease. The French made their capital at Saigon, in Vietnam, where their colonial influence was felt most strongly. Cambodia was left comparatively alone and so led an easygoing existence for the next half-century under a succession of kings of the

Modern dancers at Angkor Wat

Norodom dynasty, which is still in power in Cambodia today.

There was little evidence of Cambodian ambition or will to power for many years until the nation gained independence after World War II and found itself, because of its strategic location, involved in the worldwide struggle of the big-power blocs. Today, Cambodia's tenacity of purpose and cultural resilience are standing her in good stead as she works with great dedication on the many problems involved in building her future.

Angkor Wat

The great Angkor temples and temple-cities, impressive in their size, impressive in their beauty, stand as a historic symbol and a challenge to Cambodians today to live up to the great Khmer heritage which is theirs.

3

CAMBODIA
HAS MANY RESOURCES

There must be a strong inner core and tough resilience in the Khmer that has helped him survive and kept alive his individuality through all these centuries. For Cambodia is very near the equator, and like most tropic lands it is hot — hot twenty-four hours a day, three hundred and sixty-five days of the year. People who live constantly in such heat do not have much physical energy. The wants of people in the tropics tend to be few and quite easily satisfied. Leaders with great will to power have not risen lately to stir up the people of Cambodia, and so they are content with a simple, easygoing existence. They seem to have a vague inner awareness of their past greatness but no dynamic urge to revive it. Most of the people grow their rice and live together simply and happily in village groups. There are a few artistic people who make works in silver or carve marble or ivory, who are content to reproduce classic patterns from the past and make no effort to produce new designs. There are love of beauty and a desire to create, but the strength and motivation to develop new forms seems lacking. Although they once had great city-temples, today the Cambodians seem content with a simple village composed of a group of *paillottes*.

It is hard to analyze all the factors that have combined to make the modern Cambodians so shy and complacent, when their ancient leaders were so aggressive. But one often finds in the development of world civilizations such periods of quiescence or even regression coming after periods of aggression and of great political power. Now, however, there are many evidences that Cambodia is waking up.

With communication among all peoples of the world developing so rapidly, Cambodia, like any other nation, cannot live in isolation. The peoples of the world are increasingly interdependent. Industrialization will surely come to Cambodia, though it will come slowly, as it does to any country which is mainly agricultural to begin with. Machines, automobiles, and airplanes are a part of modern living that all the people of the world, even in agrarian countries like Cambodia, are beginning to want and use.

There are many other ways of making a living in Cambodia besides growing rice, which we have already discussed. Other resources, some of which may be used for export, are being developed. Rubber plantations flourish. Although these were mostly private enterprises prior to World War II, today new experimental farms are being developed by the government's Ministry of Agriculture. The mining of even limited resources like gold, iron, and precious stones is increasing.

Fishing is another important source of livelihood for Cambodians. All along the Mekong and its small tributary streams are situated villages whose people make their living from fishing. Most years there is even a small surplus for export. The fishing may be done in many ways — a boy may stand beside a ditch with his bamboo pole to catch a few fish, or a big business enterprise may build large weirs across a stream and net great quantities of fish.

Another common way to fish is to cast large circular nets into the river and slowly gather in the haul. Some men wade out into the river or stream and cast their own nets. Others have a double net, shaped like a butterfly, manipulated from a boat. It is beautiful to

Casting a circular fish net

A "butterfly" net

watch the net's large flare spread out, dip into the water, rise, and empty its silvery treasure; circle, dip, rise, and empty its silver, over and over and over again.

Fishing is also done with small circular traps made of bamboo that are set in the streams. When the water is high during the rainy season of the year, the catch from such traps is collected several times a day.

Much of the fish is eaten at once. Some is used to make a kind of fermented sauce, *nuoc-mam* (pronounced "nuk-mam"). There are factories which make this sauce and pack it in round clay pots for sale. The Cambodians use it for flavoring soup, vegetables, and meat, much as the Chinese use soy sauce.

A certain small silver fish is mashed and fermented into another preparation, called *prahop*, a favorite dish. In the Mekong River just

A small circular fish trap

north of the city of Phnom Penh, great schools of the small fish appear in January. At this time of the year a stretch of roadside near this spot about two miles long is lined with the oxcarts of people who have come down to catch the fish, trample the skins off in great vats, smash down the fish pulp, add a ferment, and store the result in large jars. Some simply watch the others work and then buy a large jar of *prahop* from the fishermen to take home. Hundreds of such jars are filled during the two weeks that the fish congregate at this one place on the river. When the fish have moved on, the jars are taken by oxcart to markets in every corner of the land.

Much fish is also dried and sold to other Cambodians in the markets. Nearly every Cambodian eats fish in some form — dried, fresh, or fermented — each day.

Often the people in a village concentrate on one way of making a living, and their village becomes known as a fishing village, a pot-making or dyeing village, or a gold-mining village. A Cambodian

Firing pots at Kompong Chnnang

village on the river often has as part of its name the word *kompong*, which literally means "port." Along the Mekong River north of Phnom Penh, for example, you find Kompong Chnnang, village of pots, where you see great piles of round clay pots in all sizes. Some are used to hold *nuoc-mam*, some water, some coconut milk. You also find Kompong Tralach, the village of straw-weaving, and Kompong Luong, the village where silver boxes and ornaments are made.

Inland is the village of Pursat, where most of the carving of the images is done: beautiful Buddhas, Naga heads, *apsaras*, and the four faces of Siva. Much of the carving is done in what is called Cambodian marble, a kind of soapstone, which has shades of blue-green with veins of rose or brown. Here a carver sits on the ground, holding the stone block with his toes as he chisels away. Some of the carving is done in wood, which the Cambodians as a rule stain black, covering all the original color or grain of the wood with an ebony sheen. Cambodians use black a great deal; even many of their clothes are black. Throughout the countryside you see very little color either in clothes or in anything else. A woman most often wears a black tight skirt, or *sampot*, with a black blouse.

The dye for clothes is made from the fruit of what the Cambodians call the "dye tree," a large round berry. First the long lengths of cotton or silk are dipped in the black dye and wrung out. Then four people hold the material by the corners while the wind fills it like a sail and takes out some of the moisture. After that, the cloth is spread on the ground for final drying. Dust and insects cover the wet material, but they can be shaken off, so no one minds. All around a village that specializes in dyeing you can see terraces and hillsides spread with yards of the black cloth drying in the sun.

Throughout Cambodia you see not only these little working villages but also large rubber plantations, most of them partly owned by the French. During the hundred years that Cambodia was a part of French Indochina, the French government failed to develop the country as it did Vietnam, but it did encourage the growing of rubber. The Cambodian government has continued to do so, and since

A young resident of Kompong Chnnang (village of pots)

A Pursat woodcarver

*Spreading freshly dyed
lengths of silk*

*Watering
young rubber trees
on a government
experimental farm*

The cut circling a rubber tree on a large plantation

World War II many new experimental farms have been developed by the Ministry of Agriculture. The work is done on the huge plantations by workers who live there in houses built by the owners.

A rubber plantation is an exciting and beautiful place. In a land of so much sun, it is a joy to come to a rubber plantation, with its long rows of symmetrically planted trees whose large leafy tops give welcome shade. To extract latex from the trees, a shallow cut is made in the bark circling the tree, as shown in the picture. The thick white sap trickles slowly along the half-inch groove and drips into a small bowl placed at the base. Hundreds of workers collect such bowls daily.

Across the river from Kompong Cham, the village of Chams, or Malays, is the Chup plantation, one of the largest single rubber plantations in the world. Its French directors live in villas reminiscent of the typical French colonial way of life during the last century. There are a fine clubhouse and a large tiled swimming pool for the use of the directors. These expatriates' way of life may be a lonely one at times, but it has its luxuries.

The Chup plantation is an experimental station as well as a huge growing area and production center. The finest available equipment is used to refine the rubber from crude sap to firm slabs, which are shipped to the United States to be made into tires and other rubber products. The directors have set aside many acres of young trees, where experimental grafting is done in a constant effort to develop a tree that gives a better sap.

As you drive through Cambodia, you also see many trees that have a feathery appearance. They are kapok trees, which once made a profitable export item which was used for stuffing mattresses, sofas, and many other things. The development of foam rubber and other more flexible materials for stuffing has almost closed the market for kapok. So those picturesque trees with their long pods, which are green, then brown, and then burst like milkweed pods, will be cultivated less and less and may eventually disappear from the scene.

Cambodia has many other kinds of tree that furnish hardwood

for construction and furniture-making. They grow in the hill-country rain forests, in thick jungle growths, but not in the river basin filled by the rice fields. A very durable wood called *koki* is used to make boats — the crude, rough boats seen on the rivers, which are seldom painted but are strong and adequate to get people from one place to another. It is used to make sampans, houseboats, fishing boats, and boats of all kinds. Few bridges have been built yet in this land where there are many rivers to cross, so there are many ferryboats. These are also built from *koki* wood and often have a coat of white paint. Chventeal is another local hardwood; it is much used in the increasing number of construction projects in Phnom Penh and Battambang. Wood is little used to make furniture for the villagers. The average *paillotte* contains at most a platform made from bamboo, used as a bed, and a small block of wood to sit on.

Of the trees in the Cambodian forest, the sralao is one of the most picturesque. It is tall and straight. About thirty to forty feet above ground it sends out flanges which look for all the world like flying buttresses. These tall trees provide long planks that make good hardwood floors and trimming for some of the modern villas now being built by successful businessmen in the cities.

Fire is the great enemy of the fine forests of Cambodia, just as it is in the United States. American aid is sending well-trained men from the U.S. Forestry Service to train the Cambodians in fire prevention, in planning reforestation, and in taking better care of their existing forests.

Among other Cambodian resources are the minerals of the hill country, which are not numerous but have some value. There is one large open-pit gold mine at Prek Luong, in the province of Kompong Thom. Cambodians tell tales of times past, when the gold at Prek Luong was mined secretly and smuggled out of the country. But even in this romantic land, the days of pirates and smugglers are over. About 1956 Prince Sihanouk, the present head of the government in Cambodia, authorized the working of the gold mines at Prek Luong by a cooperative group of forty-five to fifty families who now make up the village. Today, women with babies strapped to their backs and men with picks and pickaxes descend the fragile scaffolding one hundred, two hundred, three hundred feet down and chisel out chunks of the rock containing bits of gold. (There is much pyrite — so-called "fool's gold" — also. Sometimes a miner is deceived, but not for long. Experts detect it quickly.) The chunks are brought up in buckets and dumped into high round metal containers, which look like churns. The ore is pounded in the churn until the gold is separated.

Yeth and Phorium, two Cambodian girls, stand on either side of the churns with long iron rods in their hands. Thump! goes Yeth, and on her upstroke, Thump! goes Phorium.

Thump, thump! Up, down!

Thump, thump! Up, down!

Thump, thump! In perfect rhythm, they lift and pound the rocky lumps as they reduce the rocks to powder. Sometimes they pound for five minutes without stopping. Then, after a brief rest to get their breaths, it is Thump, thump! again. After half an hour they dump the pulverized pieces of rock into a basket, which Seng, a girl known as a "picker," shakes vigorously. Ah! Her practiced eye sees the shining bits of gold, which she picks out and places in a small bottle.

There are a dozen or more women and girls pounding the rock and gathering the gold into the precious little bottles. Yeth's arms ache, and so do Phorium's, but they do not complain. Seng and the other women who shake the baskets and pick out the gold bits are dust-covered and thirsty, eager to find a pail of cool water when work is done.

At the end of each day all the gold is taken to the village chief. The village is a true cooperative. Every family knows that it will receive its pro rata share of the gold. No one is rich in Prek Luong, but the income is a little better than the average in Cambodia.

Everyone has heard fantastic tales of the precious stones in the Southeast Asian lands of Burma, Ceylon, Thailand, and India.

The forest

The open pit gold mine at Prek Luong

Cambodia has a few also. The stones are concentrated in the village of Bokeo in the hills near the Vietnamese border and in the village of Paillin near the Thai border. Most of the workers in Paillin are Burmese who know precious stones well. Here there are sapphires of a deep, rich, clear blue; rubies, not the best, for they are nearer pink than red; and zircons, mostly white, but a few pale blue or pale yellow.

The process by which these exotic stones are mined is a most unusual one. A sluggish stream winds its way around hills on the outskirts of the village of Paillin. Workmen dam up pools ten or twelve feet in diameter and sit down in the water with closely woven bamboo trays in front of them. Meanwhile, their womenfolk climb up the hillside to gather bucketfuls of soft igneous rock, which is brown on the outside and slate-colored inside. They wind their way slowly down the hillside with their heavy-laden buckets. They empty them into the trays of the waiting men.

Let's watch Tek Mao. He dips his full tray in the water and shakes it from side to side. The soft muddy rock oozes out through the

Shaking the trays for sapphires at Paillin

cracks in the woven tray. He dunks and shakes his heavy tray again and again — perhaps ten times. At last there are a few hard stones left in his tray. His skilled eye searches for a blue or red or white glint among them. There is none, so he empties his tray. Another woman comes down with another load to fill his tray. Dunk, shake, dunk, shake another ten times, and he looks and looks again. Nothing! Eight trays and he is weary, but, ah! There it is, a dull blue stone. He picks out a sapphire. It does not look very bright in this unpolished state, but he knows what it is. He tucks the gem in a fold of his belt and returns to his dunking, shaking, and searching.

All day from sunrise to sunset the men sit in the muddy water, dunking, shaking, searching. All day from sunrise to sunset the women trudge up the hillsides and down with their heavy pails of muck. When it is almost five o'clock the owner comes. Tek Mao has found three stones today, one not too small. His neighbor has one, some men have two, some have none.

At the end of the day's hard work, the men and women play for awhile in the pools, but the water is so muddy that they come out still mud-covered. Discouraged? No, they talk and laugh as they walk wearily back to the village. Food is followed by sleep, and then the monotonous round begins again at dawn.

There are stone-cutters and polishers in Paillin, too. When they have done their work, the blue, blue sapphires, rosy red rubies, and sparkling zircons are shipped to the stone markets of Bangkok, Rangoon, Delhi, Paris, and New York.

Rice, fish, wood, carved soapstone, rubber, gold, precious stones — all come to your table, your home, your car, your fingers from the little tropical land of Cambodia. Look again at your new tires or your new ring, then close your eyes and see the people of Cambodia toiling in the hills and on the plains for themselves and for you.

4

THE MOUNTAINS
AND THE SEA

To know the fishing villages and the rice fields; to know the virgin forests of the hills, the alluvial plains, and the wide variety of plant life — palm and coconut trees, kapok and mango trees, banana trees, corn, pepper, cotton, sugar, indigo, rubber, and vegetables — which they support; to know the mineral resources of gold, iron, and precious stones is not to know all of Cambodia.

Cambodia is kept alive by the mighty Mekong River and by a natural fresh-water reservoir, the Tonle Sap, a great inland lake. The central part of the country is a great river basin stretching over three-quarters of Cambodia, very few parts of it more than ten feet above sea level. This is where rice is grown. To the north, near the Laotian border, are the Dangrek Mountains, largely sandstone terraces. To the east, stretching from Stung Treng to the Vietnamese border, is the Moi Plateau, some of it as high as three thousand feet. To the south and west are the Cardamon Mountains and the Elephant Mountains, "the mountains around which the clouds turn." They run right down to the Gulf of Siam, which is the southwest border of Cambodia.

These mountain areas offer a natural defense against a potential enemy. They also serve as a refuge for the dissident elements within

*Jungle at the edge
of the mountains*

the country whom the Cambodian government finds difficult to control.

A group of primitive tribes, often called the Mois, dwell in the Moi Plateau. Some Cambodians call them *Phnongs*, or savages, but they themselves resent this name. They are socially, politically, and economically outside the main stream of Cambodian life and culture. They engage in some farming and are hunters. They are vigorous and capable of great endurance, and therefore have made good guerrilla fighters.

For the most part they live apart, growing their own rice, weaving their own scant garments, and making a few baskets, crude bowls, and other necessary implements. Occasionally a foreigner may find one or two of them willing to take him on safari to hunt wild animals, but not often. They are not much interested in foreigners. The Moi people do not recognize any authority beyond that of the village chief, a man who is outstanding for his bravery and intelligence.

The Moi men wear a long *houti*, a long, narrow band of red or blue cloth wrapped several times around the waist and passed between the legs; it hangs to the ground like a queue. Members of the more advanced tribes sometimes wear a tunic jacket or small turban as well. They often let their hair grow long, braid it, and loop it up loosely.

Moi women pounding rice

Moi women and children

For skirts, the women wrap around themselves brief lengths of black cloth bordered in red or blue. Usually they wear nothing above the waist, but occasionally you see a woman in a sleeveless bodice. The Moi women love bright-colored beads, and some hang as many as a dozen chains around their necks. A village beauty like Ng Than wears ivory ear plugs. A small plug was inserted in the lobe of each ear when she was a little girl. Every year or two larger ones were inserted, and the holes were stretched until she could wear ivory plugs three inches in diameter. Such ornaments are often decorated with an etched design. Because of her beauty, Ng Than is the envy of all her village, near Bakeo. She has bands tattooed across her forehead, under her eyes, on the curve of her cheeks, and across the

Moi boy

curve of her breasts. Although she is well aware of her beauty, she is shy in the presence of strangers.

She and her brothers make bamboo pipes, sometimes three feet long, which they all enjoy smoking.

Most of Ng Than's people are superstitious. Fervent animal worshipers, they celebrate feasts and holidays by drinking much rice wine, and by singing and dancing. The men, women, and children all take part in the festivities.

There are a few mountain resort spots, such as Kerirom and Bokor, in the Elephant Mountain chain. The French once had quite a fine hotel at Bokor, which fell into disrepair after it was bombed in World War II, but plans are being made to rebuild it. With the coming of automobiles, you now see Cambodian and foreign families out picnicking at Kerirom and other attractive spots in the mountains near the streams. Here the water dashes down over the rocks from the higher mountains and offers a welcome respite from the heat of the city.

The Elephant Mountains descend to the shore of the Gulf of Siam. Here are beautiful wide, sandy beaches with shells of every shape and shade. The iridescent shells reflect the light in a thousand colors — yellow, orange, rose, and purple — that become richer in values as the clear, warm, blue-green water covers them. Some nights, tiny phosphorescent organisms seem to set aflame all the lacy

The beach at Kep

patterns of the waves as they roll in and fan out. It is as if every star were sending down a ray to light a bit of foamy water.

The swimming is good. The fishing is good. At Kep, a favorite small resort on the gulf, you can hire a fisherman to take you to one of the nearby islands, where, although there are no hotels and no modern conveniences, it is a joy to roll out a sleeping mat and sleep under the starry sky. This is life as you might dream it would be on a remote tropic isle. Here are blue waters, white sand, bending coconut palms, and one has nothing to do but enjoy them all.

There are a few fishing villages along this beautiful shore, such as Kompong Som and Ream, where the children live more in the water than out of it. Fishermen have good luck most of the time and make a good living from their catches, even hauling in enough to ship to nearby ports.

Recently, with American aid, a road a hundred and sixty miles long was built from Phnom Penh, the capital city, in the southern

The road from Phnom Penh to Sihanoukville built by Americans

part of the central basin, down to a Gulf fishing village called Sihanoukville, in honor of the prince. The French had built a breakwater and a pier there a long time ago, and a President liner once made a token stop to prove that seagoing vessels could dock there. It would be good if Cambodia could develop this village into a seaport, for now it has none. At the present time all foreign goods are sent to Saigon and are then transshipped up the Mekong to Phnom Penh — an expensive process. But to make Sihanoukville a working port, warehouses would have to be built to store shipments, and buses and trucks would have to be provided to transport people and goods a hundred and sixty miles up to Phnom Penh. One hopes that such new patterns for transportation may be developed before the road reverts to the jungle.

But changes come slowly in Cambodia. Where life is not difficult, where wants are few, where resources for shelter, clothes, and food are adequate, if not rich or varied, pressures for change are not very great.

5

PHNOM PENH,
CAPITAL OF CAMBODIA,
AND THE COUNTRY TODAY

The word *phnom* means "hill" in the Khmer language (the "h" is silent as it so often is in Khmer words). *Penh* was the family name of a wealthy lady of ancient times. (It is pronounced as if it were spelled "peng" — almost, but not quite. Do not make the "ng" ring.) The legend goes that when the gods answered the lady's prayers she built a shrine on a hill, which came to be known as the hill of the lady Penh — Phnom Penh.

The hill and its city are on the banks of the Mekong River, near the place where the waters from the Great Lake, Tonle Sap, flow into the Mekong. The water forms itself into four arms at the junction. The French called this meeting place of the waters "Quatre Bras," or Four Arms, and it is so called by almost everyone. It was natural for a village located at so strategic a point near the center of the great central basin to develop into the capital and largest city (population 500,000) of Cambodia.

The hill, with its shrine, is at the north end of the main part of the city. From it the main thoroughfare, Norodom Street, which is named for the royal family, stretches for about two miles to a monument which commemorates the independence Cambodia gained after World War II. It is a wide street, lined with government

The phnom with its shrine

buildings, schools, banks, and villas belonging to wealthy citizens. The buildings are all of stucco, most of them a yellowish beige color. Some have small enclosed yards in which one sees tropical flowers: bougainvillaea, hibiscus, poinsettia, frangipani. These look especially beautiful, for there are very few flowers in Cambodia, even in the villages or countryside. Perhaps this is due to the long dry season of six or seven months. But there is a general lack of color anywhere in the country; there are few flowers, few birds, and few brightly colored clothes. Blue sky, blue water, green rice, and flaming sunsets provide the only color.

The section of the city which lies between Norodom Street and the Mekong River is the section where the Chinese live and conduct

A group of Chinese students

their business. It is Phnom Penh's Chinatown. Its buildings are also stuccoed, but they are smaller and built right up to the edge of the sidewalk. Here you see school children in their school uniforms — girls with white blouses and dark blue skirts, boys with white shirts and short khaki pants. They look clean, well fed, and alert. Shop fronts are open, and much business is done on the sidewalk. Family life goes on inside and outside. The grandmothers wear trousers and the traditional Chinese garb. The younger women sometimes wear Chinese-cut robes of lovely silk, sometimes Western dress. The older men wear black Chinese silk robes, but nearly all the younger men wear Western shorts, or trousers and shirts. All of them are clean and active. They conduct much of the business of this country. They handle the large traffic on the river, they sell vegetables in the market, they do many other kinds of work.

76   CAMBODIA

It is interesting to note the number of schools in the Chinese sector of Phnom Penh that are called "Practical English School" or "Practical English College." Like the Cambodians, Vietnamese, Thais, Malayans, and Indonesians, the Chinese sense that English is replacing French as the language of international communication. They are eager to learn it.

The Chinese people are not newcomers to Cambodia. They have been in the country for four, five, or six generations, as they have been in all the countries of Southeast Asia. But they remain Chinese in their hearts and in their ways.

The Chinese in Phnom Penh do not talk much about communism or Red China; they also say very little about Nationalist China. But they eagerly read books about life in China today and buy cards showing pictures of life there as well as reproductions of old

Unloading boats up the steep concrete slope of the river bank in Phnom Penh

ceramics, forms of art which are shipped down from Hong Kong and from Peiping and other Chinese cities. These expatriate Chinese control the economic life of Southeast Asia. They stay closely together in family groups. The Chinese people in Phnom Penh are a highly disciplined, hard-working portion of the population.

The river bank of Phnom Penh is covered with concrete that slopes down to the water's edge and runs along most of the length of the city. Ships ply the waters along its banks. Produce from the surrounding countryside arrives daily in small boats and is carried up the steep, smooth slope by bearers with heavy baskets on each end of the poles slung over their shoulders. Gravel for construction also arrives in small boats and is carried up the slope in baskets. The bearers seem tireless as they carry heavy burdens from the boats up the slope to market again and again and again.

Ferryboats go back and forth across the river to the small villages on the bank opposite the city. The boats are laden with people, with bicycles, and with large baskets of fish, onions, bananas, and crockery. A passenger jumps over the side into the ferry and scrambles to find a place to sit or stand. No Cambodian pays much attention to other Cambodians. They may watch a foreigner but seldom offer help. The Cambodians are shy as well as self-sufficient.

It is fun to take a ferry over to a village on the far bank of the Mekong and walk about a mile to the home of the best maker of drums. He supplies orchestras and bands with drums of all kinds. He makes them by hollowing lengths of log, from eighteen inches to three feet long, and shaping them gracefully, rather like vases. Then he stretches snakeskin or pigskin across the tops to make fine two-toned drums, the tone depending on how tightly the drummer holds the edge.

When the ferry comes back across to the river embankment, you see boys carrying fish or fruit or rocks up the steep slope of concrete. They are barefoot, of course, but they know how to curl their toes to take hold. There are food vendors, some with tiny fires, selling rice and fish, others with two-wheeled carts, selling soft drinks (not

Gateway to the Royal Palace

iced). There are small girls with baskets on their heads full of small peeled chunks of sugar cane for sale. There are groups of little children running up and down or sitting with their mothers, watching the boats on the river. You see many cyclos, those three-wheeled bicycle rickshas with their drivers, the cyclo boys, looking eagerly for customers. People, people, people! There is more activity along the crowded river bank than in almost any other part of the city.

Near the middle of the two-mile length of the embankment are the small gilded boathouses of the royal family. Above the bank is a large square park, and, in back of that, the Royal Palace. A high wall with a handsome gate in front surrounds the palace grounds. Near it is a booth where pictures of events past and present are posted, as well as current news items. There are always people standing in the booth studying the pictures and reading the news.

Armed guards stand watch at the palace gates, and only those

The royal elephants near the palace

people with official business may enter the grounds, except on Sunday mornings, when any visitor may go in. The Royal Palace has a gilded tile roof and winged, up-curled projections at each corner. Many people who have never visited Cambodia before think that all Cambodian houses are like this. It is a surprise to find that only the Royal Palace is so picturesque.

Several buildings on the palace grounds have handsome reception rooms, one with a floor of silver. On one side of the palace grounds are the stables, where the royal white elephant is kept. Children love to watch the elephant, which gets out on parade only occasionally.

The royal Norodom family lives in the palace. Prince Norodom Sihanouk is the head of the government, which is a limited constitutional monarchy. There is a house of elected representatives, the National Assembly. There are Ministries of Information, Foreign

A dancer of the Royal Palace

Affairs, Education, Health, and Agriculture; the chief ministers form
a council or cabinet. Shifts in government are frequent, and there is
no secure sense of government controls. However, there is one day
each year when anyone who has a grievance may go to the grounds
of the Royal Palace and be heard, and many hundreds do come to

be heard. The grievances are generally petty ones, but the Cambodians enjoy seeing their prince and being part of a big crowd.

One of the most fascinating groups living at the palace are the royal dancers. The carefully selected members of this group are trained from early childhood to perform the slow-moving, graceful ancient Cambodian dances. Their costumes of brocade and gold are gorgeous to behold, but they dance only for the royal family and its guests. The dances are traditional, often dramatizing old Cambodian folk tales. The movements are slow and highly stylized, with graceful use of the fingers and hands, demanding the superb control that results from years of training and discipline. Once a year, at New Year's time, this group of beautiful girls is taken up to Angkor Wat for a traditional celebration. Looking at the exquisitely carved *apsaras* on the walls of the ancient temples and then turning to watch the exquisite movements of these golden girls, you get a vivid sense of the continuous cultural pattern of the Khmer people.

The royal family is a large and colorful one. Sihanouk's mother and sisters and his courtiers attend numerous social functions, including many of those given by the American, British, and Indian colonies in Phnom Penh.

For many reasons, as we said briefly in Chapter 2, the ancient Khmer civilization which flourished so magnificently from 800 to 1400 A.D. began to disintegrate in the fifteenth century. Finally, when it faced a threat of invasion by its neighbors in the middle of the nineteenth century, Cambodia asked France to incorporate it in the French colonial system. Laos and Vietnam also feared the Siamese and did the same. So these three countries became French Indochina, a French colony. The French set up the capital at Saigon, a charming city in Vietnam with wide, tree-lined avenues, large government buildings, and handsome shops and restaurants. But the countries of Cambodia and Laos were considered hinterland, and little attention was paid to their needs or special interests. Being naturally easygoing, the people demanded little, so very little was done for them.

The royal family inside the palace

A few schools were established, but attendance was not required. The highest school was the lycée, and there was only one in Cambodia. It was academically at about the level of the first two years of college in the United States and had perhaps fifty students a year. Life was simple in Cambodia during that time. Contacts with the outside world were few.

Then, in 1954, the three countries won complete independence from France, and Cambodia set about establishing its own government, educating its people, struggling to make itself into a modern nation. With extremely limited resources, both human and natural, with practically no industrial base, with untrained leadership in almost every significant area of modern life and no training facilities, the government of Cambodia began working with great dedication to solve its almost insurmountable problems.

One of the great problems has been that of improving education.

The methods of teaching in the lower schools need to be modernized. As more children attend school and become interested in going on to high school and the lycée, extra high schools have to be provided. Then there is the task of finding enough white-collar jobs for those who get a higher education and who are no longer content to stay in the rice villages. As industrialization increases and transportation improves, facilities to train engineers, machinists, and fliers must be developed. All the agencies of the Cambodian government need strengthening to carry this out.

The leadership group of trained teachers, engineers, lawyers, and ministers is small. One man with training does the work of three or four. A few of these men have been educated in Europe, but only a very few. The disparity in training between the few fully educated Cambodians and the many uneducated ones is another reason why this is often called a land of extreme opposites, a land of great contrasts.

For centuries Cambodia's foreign relations were mainly with its neighbors: Vietnam, Laos, Thailand, Burma, Malaya, and Indonesia. But today its relations extend to countries throughout the world. These increasing contacts with remote countries have brought about more pressure for change, and many of Cambodia's overseas friends are offering her aid.

Great Britain, through the Colombo Plan, is helping solve the country's education problem, especially by providing well-trained teachers for secondary schools. Britain is also helping train young men for the Cambodian diplomatic service.

Japan is building a water system for the huge sprawling city of Phnom Penh. Mainland China is building paper and plywood factories, much needed by an industry that will become increasingly important as more people learn to read and write and so want more books and writing materials.

The Soviet Union is providing a well-equipped, well-staffed hospital as well as some school buildings and language-teaching centers.

India is giving military aid and guidance.

The United States has developed an ambitious program of aid through both private and government channels. The Asia Foundation, a private organization, offers help in education; it provides scholarships to the Buddhist Institute in Phnom Penh, tape recorders and machines to record ancient folk music, and help in other education projects.

The United States Government offers the communication facilities of the United States Information Service, known as U.S.I.S. The United States foreign-aid program is carried out by an agency of the state department, the Agency for International Development. Assistance is offered in eight areas: military, public works, police, health, education, agriculture, public administration, and small industries. One example: Under the Smith-Mundt Plan, the U.S. sends teachers for Cambodian secondary schools.

The United Nations Educational, Scientific and Cultural Organization (UNESCO) and the World Health Organization offer aid to health and education. Among other things, they send school nurses, establish maternity centers, initiate training of midwives, and supply dried milk and other commodities.

Deciding how to utilize all this aid to the best advantage presents Cambodia with a serious problem. But Cambodia's foreign friends have an equally big problem in settling on the right kind of aid to give the country. The Cambodians, ideally, should have the sort of aid which would give them what they need and want of Western culture but would at the same time preserve what is beautiful and good in their own.

The educated Cambodians who live and work in Phnom Penh are only a tiny part of the city's total population. Most of them live on Norodom Street and a few side streets in two- or three-storied buildings. But huddled beside them and spreading out all over the sprawling city are small *paillottes*, similar to the ones seen in the rice villages. Here most of the people live in great simplicity, with few possessions, few wants, little knowledge, and little privacy. They live simply, but they are not primitive — not in the sense that the Maoris of New Zealand, for instance, are primitive.

That the Cambodians' ancient culture once reached great heights is evidenced by the ruins of Angkor Wat and by the Khmer treasures in the Royal Museum beside the palace. Inside the museum are many ancient stone carvings of gods and people, some very interesting old bowls and vases, and many metal implements. The Cambodians' interest and skill in ceramics and metals were once highly developed. Attached to the museum is a school of the arts, where a small group of eager boys is learning to carve both native marble and wood; to make silver bowls, plates, spoons, forks, tiny boxes to hold betel nuts, bracelets, earrings, necklaces, and rings; to construct musical instruments such as marimbas, drums, and cymbals; to do cutout designs on pigskin; and to make masks for special plays and dances.

The designs and techniques have been handed down from generation to generation, but the standards have declined in many ways. The quality of the silver work is not as high as it was. Almost no work is now done in ceramics; crude clay water pots are produced up-country in quantity but are made with no artistic merit.

Nonetheless, the old Khmer designs and techniques *do* persist. The efforts of seemingly stronger cultures to conquer the Khmers developed a kind of strength and durability in these gentle people. And this strength may partly explain the fact that the Khmer ways are still followed, that the Khmer language is still used, and that the Khmers believe they can survive as an independent Cambodian nation.

Politically the Cambodians would like to remain neutral. What they have observed of Western civilization does not make them eager to take on all Western ways. They would like to select from the West only what they feel they want. They continue to resist the outside Oriental cultures as well, as they have for centuries. Partly as a result, although there is a royal school of administration, its standards and training seem inadequate by Western standards, as do those of the small lycée.

The stupas near the Royal Palace

There are many Buddhist *wats,* with their connected schools, throughout the city of Phnom Penh. Not far from the palace is the Buddhist Institute for higher education, but its faculty is not very well trained. It has a library, but it is a small one; and because the books are all about Buddha and written in ancient script, they are wholly inadequate for modern learning.

In one of the large Buddhist *wats* not far from the Royal Palace, on a canopy-covered platform, the cremation of royal and important people takes place. (All Cambodians are cremated after death, so there are no cemeteries.) Around this *wat* stand many small towers, or *stupas,* of various shapes and sizes. These hold the ashes of distinguished people.

The whole pattern of Cambodian life is determined by the Buddhist religion. Since Buddhists believe in reincarnation, there is no compulsion to get anything accomplished in a hurry. If they don't finish a task in this life, Buddhists expect to do it in the next. Thus

The funeral procession of an important Cambodian official

Decorating the framework around the platform for a cremation

death is actually another birth and is not feared as much as it is in most of the Western world. Buddhist funerals are colorful, accompanied by offerings of flowers, food, and incense to make the soul's journey more comfortable. Added to a climate that is always hot, the Buddhist philosophy produces a slow, casual way of life.

Tensions and pressures are few in Cambodia. So are instances of nervous disorders and of many of the so-called "civilization diseases" such as cancer, arthritis, and heart ailments. Cambodia needs help from the West in obtaining pure water, better hospitals, better homes, and better schools, but it also has much to give to the people of the Western world. Perhaps our twentieth-century world civilization will have a better chance of survival if we as individuals as well as nations can bring ourselves to learn as well as teach, to take as well as give.

6

LIFE IN PHNOM PENH

Although about 85 per cent of all the inhabitants of Cambodia are Khmer, or Cambodian, in the city of Phnom Penh only about 42 per cent are Khmer. Thirty per cent are Chinese, 27 per cent Vietnamese, and 1 per cent other nationalities.

Cambodia is one of the few countries of Asia that is not overpopulated. There is enough food in the city as well as the country — rice, vegetables, fruit, and fish — to feed everyone, so there is no starvation and little begging, in contrast, for example, with South India. No one has very much, but everyone has enough for survival. The number of wealthy people is very small.

Ninety-five per cent of all Cambodians are Buddhists. In Phnom Penh there are a few Catholics among the Vietnamese, and a few Moslems among the Malayans. It is the Malayans who are the butchers for Cambodia. They prepare the small amount of beef and pork that is available. Buddhists are not permitted to take life, but some eat meat if they can afford it.

Every street in Phnom Penh is a busy place. Most of the houses are so small that the inhabitants spend their waking hours in the streets. Children play there. Women talk to each other there about children and food, sitting there for hours on their haunches. All kinds

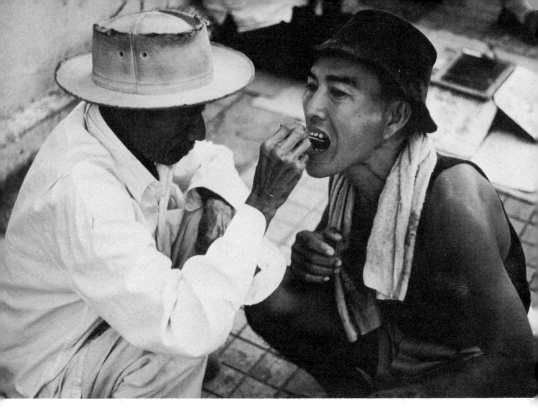

A sidewalk dentist

of business goes on, as much on the sidewalks or in the streets as in the open-front shops. Along the sidewalk on one block are the barbers. A pair of scissors, a mirror, and a small box for the customer to sit on, and a "shop" is ready for business. Along the sidewalks on other blocks are the dentists. Again a small box (not absolutely essential; it is just about as easy to sit on the ground) plus a pair of forceps, and the dentist is ready to pull that aching tooth. Sometimes he does not even own the tweezers but borrows a pair from a neighbor. There is no running water here with which to rinse your mouth, so you spit out the saliva and blood right there, as others do whenever they feel like it. It is behavior like this that disturbs Western people. If the dentist has been in business for some years, he may have a few gold caps to sell to cover a tooth, or a row of six to cover six front teeth. This is one way to store one's wealth. Occasionally

LIFE IN PHNOM PENH   91

A "wealthy" young man

A water cart

that golden tooth covering may have a sapphire or diamond set in it, and this is a sign of real wealth.

There is little running water in Phnom Penh except in foreign-built homes and business buildings. This is piped from the Mekong River and filtered many times. The majority of Cambodians buy their water from water boys, however. There are water plugs at various places in the city to supply them. There is one near the Royal Hotel.

At five o'clock in the morning, hundreds of water carts on two wheels are parked for blocks around that plug. The water boys are asleep under their carts (round water kegs on wheels) or in nearby trees. Everything is very still in the early dawn. About six o'clock, the red sun begins to show over the horizon. A few dogs bark. The city water man appears and opens the plug.

Splash — the sound of gushing water!

The boys wake up and run toward the plug. Those first in line are lucky. They run into the gushing stream of water (their best chance for a bath), then jump out, and roll their water kegs up to be filled.

As each keg is filled, into it goes a stopper, and off to his own block trots the water boy to sell the precious water. He sets himself up on a corner, often on a small wooden platform, and is open for business. Children come with one- or two-gallon cans to buy the precious water.

When his keg is empty, the water boy picks up the shafts that hold the keg and pull the wheels, and trots back to refill his keg. He may do this three or four times during the day. The water gushes from the water plug like a fountain every day as the boys fill and refill their water carts.

Pure water is considered one of the great needs of this land. The Cambodians hope that the water system the Japanese are installing in Phnom Penh, in payment of war reparations, will be the beginning of a complete city-wide water system for the big sprawling capital of a half-million inhabitants.

In the streets of Phnom Penh there are peddlers of everything from tiny cheap plastic toys to carved ivory beads or statues of the Buddha. As in the rice villages, there are food vendors everywhere.

Some of the vendors deal in specialties, such as peeled chunks of sugar cane, sections of watermelon or papaya, fried bananas, broiled sparrows, or tarantulas fried in deep fat. There are soft drinks, too, especially an orange drink called Green Spot, and there is always coconut milk. None of these is cold, for there is little ice available.

Everyone is friendly and looks happy. The children, the men and women, the hard-working water boys and peddlers with heavy loads, — all seem interested in what goes on. Children learn much from being part of all the life in the streets of the city.

For those who sell in the markets, the day begins early, about five in the morning. There are several markets under rough shelter in various parts of the city, occupying a square block or more apiece. The large central market is about half a mile square, most of it under a roof; but the green-vegetable sellers spill out into the open, pouring water over their vegetables to keep things looking fresh and putting up huge umbrellas to shield their wares from the burning sun.

In the stillness of the hour before dawn there is nothing in the market, but soon almost every square inch is covered with fresh foods and merchandise, children, sellers, and buyers — all of them shouting, bargaining, jostling, pushing, or making way for a child to sleep on a counter or floor. In the city just as in the villages, hand-carts and oxcarts filled with vegetables and fruit begin to roll into the city long before dawn. Cyclos and small cars bring baskets and boxes of fish and of meat. Carts pulled by oxen come laden with so many pots that you cannot see the cart underneath. Men under mounds of baskets come trotting in. (It seems to lighten the burden to trot with it rather than to walk or run.)

The market is divided into sections; all the fish is taken to one area, the meat to another. Vegetables are laid out in baskets or in piles. The fruit — bananas, papaya, *pamplemousse* (grapefruit), and oranges — is in baskets, too, the better grades inside the shelters. Here the merchant may arrange the oranges in neat piles.

*The market
at its peak*

*The great
central market*

The early customers, many of them the servants of foreigners or wealthy Cambodians, arrive by five o'clock. They want the pick of the shrimp or lobster, the freshest beans, the best papaya. By seven o'clock half the merchandise is sold, and the market is so crowded that one can hardly walk. By ten o'clock all the best merchandise is gone, and by noon the sellers are cleaning up and returning to the country. A quiet falls over the market, and only a few vendors who sell pots and baskets and less perishable items like oranges are still around.

Every day the markets come alive, flourish, and decline like this — the great central market of Phnom Penh, the dozen or more smaller ones scattered over the city, and the hundreds scattered in villages over the country.

The Chinese market in Phnom Penh is cleaner and more orderly than the others. It is all under a roof with well-marked aisles. There are pears and peaches and plums imported from Japan and Australia. Everything costs a little more here, but it is worth the difference.

Surrounding all the markets are cloth shops with hundreds of bolts of material piled high, a few of them unfolded to show their special color or texture and lure in customers. Side by side are crockery and hardware shops, most of them selling cheap merchandise from China. In between are jewelry shops, many with golden chains and rings, bracelets and anklets, all in the unusual orange-tinted gold preferred by Orientals.

All the better shops are in the Chinese section of the city. Here you find dishes, hardware, cloth, watches, and medications. Along the waterfront you can buy rope and rice mats and baskets. Along one block, men from East India sell cotton cloth and a few silk saris and delicate scarves.

Near the museum there is a street known as Silver Street, scarcely a block long. Here are the shops of a few families who sell the typical Cambodian silver bowls and plates, pepper grinders, spoons and forks, rings and bracelets, and boxes that are square or round or

Selling corn at a smaller market

shaped like a pineapple, duck, or monkey. All of these articles are hammered out in intricate designs, that have been handed down from one generation to another. Most of the silver is very thin and has been molded over a piece of not-too-hard resin. Then the design is traced on the silver and laboriously tapped out. As a result, the design stands out like a bas-relief. Often the silver worker rubs a little black soot into the depressed parts. He seems to prefer his silver darkened rather than bright and shiny. A large silver bowl, urn, or goblet with a bas-relief design is a favorite wedding gift for people who can afford it. For many years the Paong family has been making beautiful silver objects on Silver Street. The Paongs are very gifted, and their work is especially pleasing to foreigners because of its high quality.

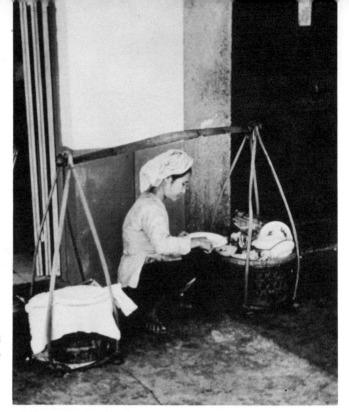

A one-woman restaurant

A sidewalk restaurant

An oxcart on its way to the city market

There is a restaurant on almost every corner of the city, tables and chairs filling the sidewalks. By nine o'clock in the morning, the tables are filled with men drinking tea or coffee, smoking and talking. What a listening post! Here is a place where you can learn what is really going on in Cambodia, Laos, Vietnam, or sometimes even China.

As we have said, in Cambodia a restaurant may be anything from one person with his baskets slung over his shoulder on a pole to a large Chinese restaurant. There are also a few French restaurants still surviving in Phnom Penh and there are good ones in the city's hotels. The Chinese food there is varied and popular with foreigners as well as Chinese. And the French onion soup, in a clay bowl topped with a round of toast covered with cheese, and put under the broiler for a few minutes, is as good as any you can get in France.

A bus loading for a trip

The best hotel in Phnom Penh, the Rajah, has an excellent restaurant with a charming terrace surrounded by palms, hibiscus, and frangipani. There one may enjoy a cheese soufflé, shrimp, lobster, or a pepper steak (green peppercorns cooked and put over broiled steak), and have baked Alaska for dessert. Few Cambodians dine there, however, or would know much about such food. The restaurant chiefly serves foreign guests.

On the edge of town stands a building made of tin and wood that houses a night club. Attended mostly by young people, it features a good Philippine orchestra that plays modern dance music. The guests sit at tables around the dance floor, drink soft drinks, eat a little something, and enjoy the dancing. Cambodians love best their

Cyclo for hire

lamthon dance, but they are now learning the rhumba, the cha-cha, and the tango. Western influences are creeping into the dances, and the young people are interested and delighted by this.

The means of transportation in Phnom Penh are as varied as the ways of eating. Both oxcarts and airplanes have their place. Crude carts pulled by oxen take people, pots, baskets, and vegetables from nearby country villages to the city markets. Large buses travel the few bumpy roads that cross the countryside. The seats slide from one side of the bus to the other. The seats are built for six passengers, but ten to twelve of the slim little Cambodians can crowd onto them. A dozen people hang on behind the bus. Bicycles, baskets of vegetables, and a few boys are piled on top. It is amazing to see all that one Cambodian bus can carry as it lumbers along the roads and city streets.

In some country villages and all over Phnom Penh you see cyclos with their gay, eager drivers. Often the cyclo is its driver's sole possession in life and only home. The vehicle has a low-slung seat holding one passenger, large wheels on either side, and a large wheel in the rear surmounted by a seat where the driver sits and pedals his riders to their destination. He will drive you to and from market or anywhere for a few riels. Thirty-five riels are equal to one dollar.

There are a few automobiles in Phnom Penh, but the number is gradually increasing. At the licensing bureau, you can see crowds of boys eager to apply for drivers' licenses. Most of the cars are small European makes; the Volkswagen is the most popular.

Phnom Penh has a modern airport. Planes from Hong Kong, Saigon, and Bangkok, and jets from Paris, Rome, and Calcutta stop there regularly.

There are only a few trained Cambodian fliers at present, but many boys are eager to learn and will probably do so in the near future. As the world draws closer together and countries exchange goods, ideas, and customs, the people change. Cambodians will change too, keeping many of their old ways but learning new ones to keep pace with a world in transition.

7

HOLIDAYS
AROUND THE YEAR

In Cambodia, as in most of the world, the cycle of the year moves from one holiday to the next. Some are religious, some are national — all of them reflections of the cultural values of the people. Everyone in Cambodia loves a holiday, and all through the country villages, towns, and cities give themselves up wholeheartedly to each celebration.

The year opens with Tet, the Chinese New Year. Even in Cambodia, this is one of the most exciting seasons of the year. Three days in late January are officially given over to its celebration, but preparations begin weeks in advance, and the actual celebrating often goes on for a whole week.

Early in January decorations go up in the markets, shops, and streets. Flowers and flowering potted plants appear by the hundreds, as they do before Easter in the United States. Most significant are the hundreds and hundreds of Tet trees. A Tet tree is a branch of a yellow flowering shrub not unlike our forsythia. If a Tet tree bursts into bloom on the first day of Tet, its owner or owners will have good luck during all the coming year. Thus the growers and sellers have many tricks to force the bloom at the right moment. Those with buds about to burst bring a very high price on the eve of Tet.

*All dressed up
for Tet*

Part of a Tet parade

Not only does every Chinese family and every Chinese shop display a Tet tree, but Cambodians, Vietnamese, and people in the foreign colonies all buy them too.

Children are given all kinds of gifts, toys, and noisemakers at Tet time and make the most of every opportunity to have fun during these days. There are new clothes for many in the family. Families call on each other. Of course, all shops are closed. Business is at a standstill as people prepare for the New Year ahead. It is a time for making brave new resolutions, forgiving debts, and raising money for the needy.

One of the most exciting means of obtaining money for the poor is by "Raising the Dragon." A large paper dragon is held on a stick by several boys. Drummers and musicians take their place under the balcony of a house and begin to play. Slowly the dragon rears his head to the second-story balcony. Excited crowds watch and cheer as members of the family come out on the balcony and put money for charity into the mouth of the dragon. The musicians drum the dragon down and move on to the next prospect. Crowds of children follow the dragon as he goes up to the balcony of one home after another. A lot of money is raised in this dramatic way, and what fun the boys have in the process!

Musicians in a Tet parade

Other parades march down the streets. Colorful costumes, dragons, animals, flowers, gongs, and drums all chase out the demons of
the past year and welcome in the favorable spirits of the new. The
slate is clean. Golden opportunity lies ahead.

The scribes on every street are busy writing good wishes and
prayers on pieces of bright red paper for their customers to give to
friends. With a flourish, their long brushes make the beautiful Chinese characters for Health, Long Life, Good Luck, Prosperity. Small
pieces of thin red paper with a character written in black sell for
half a riel or less. Elaborate scrolls with the wishes painted in gold
leaf cost many riels. The scrolls and prayers are hung either outside
a house or shop on either side of the door or gate, or on the inside.

A "Happy New Year" is expressed to friends and family all over
the world, but nowhere more colorfully than by the Chinese celebration of Tet.

Toward the end of February comes the Buddhist All Saints' Day.
There are so many Buddhists in Cambodia that this holiday is widely
observed, with special presentation of gifts and prayers to the Buddha for the welfare of all souls. Crowds gather in the temple courtyards, and there is much gaiety and feasting as well as praying.

The three-day Cambodian New Year celebration comes in April.
There are also feasts and small parades, but this is not as colorful or
elaborate a holiday as the Chinese Tet. Each celebration seems characteristic of the people. It is interesting to observe the mutual respect of these two different nationalities, the Cambodian and the
Chinese, so different in temperament and in customs, and to realize
the extent to which they live harmoniously side by side in the same
city — each following his own cultural pattern.

Another special Buddhist festival comes in May, when people go
to the *wats* for two or three days of praying, presenting gifts, and
gay feasting. Food vendors are everywhere. Families camp on the
ground, either in the temple yards or nearby. *Bonzes* move among
them in their saffron-colored robes. Youth groups put up exhibits of
their activities.

A Chinese scribe writing the good wishes for health, long life, good luck
and prosperity to be given to friends during Tet

In early October the Chinese celebrate a Festival of Ancestors which makes Westerners think of Hallowe'en. Weeks before this holiday one can buy packs of paper with bits of silver or gold leaf on each small sheet. This is spirit money. On the afternoon of the first day of the festival all Chinese shops are closed. Feasts for the souls of the ancestors are spread on tables in the front of the open shops or on the sidewalk. Chicken, duck, shrimp, fish, rice, vegetables — all of this food is on handsome platters and in beautiful

In the courtyard of a wat a family makes preparations for receiving guests during a festival

china bowls. Several candlesticks surround each feast with lighted candles, and there are flowers and burning sticks of punk. Toward sundown small fires are built at the edge of the sidewalk, and the spirit money is put into them so that the ancestors will have the wherewithal to travel on their way. Late that night the feasts disappear. It is not hard to guess who eats all that good food.

Just as we do, the Cambodians celebrate national holidays: the King's Anniversary in March, Constitution Day on May 6, Independence Day on November 9, and Human Rights Day on December 10. Each of these is a legal holiday, celebrated with appropriate ceremonies, including parades and speeches — very like our own Washington's Birthday and Fourth of July celebrations.

It is interesting to discover how many old ways and habits survive in the Cambodians' life alongside modern ways and new procedures. Some of the old ways seem superstitious and surprising to us. For instance, many Cambodians still consult astrologers to set the most auspicious hour for a wedding or other important occasion. Old customs are also seen to survive in Cambodian festivals.

One such festival that must go very far back in time is the Plowing of the Royal Furrow, which still takes place late each May in the courtyard of the Royal Palace. The holiday comes at the beginning of the rainy season, when the rice fields are being planted and everyone is anxiously wondering whether it will be a productive season. Will there be enough rain? Will the rice harvest be good?

A bowl of rice, a bowl of water, and an empty bowl are placed on the ground. Carefully selected bulls are led to the area where the bowls are placed; then the bulls are released. If they go to the bowl filled with water, there will be a good rainfall. If they go to the bowl filled with rice, there will be a good harvest. But, alas! If they sniff at the empty bowl, this will be a year of poor harvest and little grain.

Even today, when the Cambodians are getting more scientific knowledge about the weather and agriculture, crowds of people gather early in the morning to watch this ceremony.

The climax of the year's holidays in Cambodia is the Water Festival in early November. The exact dates are set by ritual to begin on the first day of full moon in the month of Katlik. The time comes close to the end of the flood season, when Cambodia lies under the immense lakes that are formed as the mighty Mekong overflows its banks. The exact origin of this festival is not clear, but it is probably associated with the early Cambodians' desire to give thanks to water and earth for their benefits and to propitiate both water and earth gods and spirits.

From May to November, as the snows of the mountains to the north melt and the rains fall, the Mekong rises to flood stages, depositing rich silt over the flat land. It flows southward to the South China Sea. In November, at the peak of the flood, a strange phenomenon occurs. The current reverses itself, and water flows northward to the Tonle Sap, the great lake, for a short period. Later, as the waters subside, the current resumes its normal southward course to the sea.

Both the reversal and the subsequent resumption of normal flow

The Royal Boathouse at the water festival

take place at Quatre Bras, the junction of lake and river near Phnom Penh.

All through the moist summer months the rice has been ripening and the concern of the people for a good harvest has mounted and mounted. Because the agricultural rhythm follows the rhythm of the annual floods, the Khmers have sought from the most ancient days to please the river gods. If the river gods looked upon the river men with favor, the Cambodians prospered and the rice crop was good.

The festival which honors these river gods lasts for three days and nights, during which no one works. All the people in the city of Phnom Penh, plus the thousands who come in from villages and all those who live along the river, crowd the embankments to watch the floats by night and the *pirogue*-racing all day.

The *pirogue*-racing is the most popular event of the three-day festival. The King has special floating barges built beside his boathouse in front of the Royal Palace. Invitations to sit in these excellent seats are a coveted honor.

The pirogues gather for the water-festival race

A *pirogue* is a large dugout canoe. Each village builds its own and trains its rowers for the race. The canoes are stored in village pagodas during the year, and their launching each November for the Water Festival is an elaborate traditional ceremony. First a fresh coat of paint is given each canoe, then eyes are painted on either side of the prow. Once it has eyes, each boat is believed to possess a spiritual personality.

Village men practice their rowing for weeks before the festival. Only the most adept are chosen, usually about thirty or forty to a boat. If the village is prosperous, its inhabitants make gaily colored costumed for those who are selected. Once the eyes have invested the *pirogue* with its own personality and once the rowers have been chosen, every hour of practice is business as serious as a temple ritual. On the first day of the festival the whole village goes down to the shore to see their boat or boats launched, and when it is time for the race nearly a hundred *pirogues* gather a half-mile or so upriver from the royal floating barges.

The rowers are seated, except for the few Moslems, who always row from a standing position. One man in each boat is leader; he is specially dressed in a silk costume and carries a short red-and-gold-lacquered paddle to mark the rhythm for his crew. Gay tassels are fastened in front of the *pirogue* to ward off evil spirits. The helmsman maintains the course in the stern with a free oar.

Almost every *pirogue* contains one or two clowns. Their faces are gaily painted or covered with masks. The clowns help to mark the rowers' rhythm, but they also joke and sing popular chants. Some are familiar to the watching crowds. A skillful clown makes up spontaneous comic verses to the popular chants, poking fun at the girls, perhaps, but always being careful not to offend the river spirits. The clowns' sharp, pungent wit keeps the rowers active, distracts competing *pirogues,* and entertains the watching crowds.

Two by two the *pirogues* race the kilometer distance from the starting point to the royal barge. Two *pirogues,* with a rope stretched between them, are anchored on either side of the course to mark the finish line, and two men robed in brilliant red act as judges. Thousands watch these races, reveling in the skill of the rowers and the wit of the clowns.

At night fifteen to twenty large electrically illuminated floats slowly sail along the river, depicting various aspects of Cambodian life. One may be shaped like a fish; another, like a cornucopia filled with fruit; still others, like snake heads or the gateways to a courtyard. Various business enterprises and government organizations sponsor these floats.

The three days of the festival are filled with revelry and fun. The river banks are crowded with thousands of people, day and night.

Floats for the water festival

And on the last evening of the festival, the *pirogues* all row upriver for a final race. A leather cord is stretched across the river, behind which all the *pirogues* are gathered. Excitement runs high.

Suddenly a man known as a *bakou*, with a saber in his hand, appears in the prow of a canoe rowed by seven men.

He approaches the cord. Shouts go up. He hesitates, draws back, moves forward, hesitates, draws back, moves forward. The shouting diminishes as the watching crowd holds its breath. The *bakou* slashes the cord and orders his canoe to flee.

"The signal! The signal!" The crowd cheers and cheers.

All the *pirogues* leap forward in this final race to the royal barge of Their Majesties, the King and Queen. The winner receives due homage, but every *pirogue* shares in the honors of this festival, for everyone has done his part in contributing to the gala spectacle.

Now several *bakous* in brocaded red and gold garments approach His Majesty, the King. They present him with a giant sea shell filled with water drawn from the river. The King sprinkles his hair and face with this water and salutes the moon as it appears over the horizon.

Once again the life-giving waters of the Mekong assure enough to eat for the coming year to all who dwell in the good land of Cambodia.

The floats sail away. The moon rises, changing from a copper ball to a silver one. The stars fill the heavens. The crowds begin to disperse — but slowly, for a festival like this one comes only once a year, and no one wants it to end.

The excitement dies down. Cyclos roll away in all directions. Overloaded buses start up-country to far villages. Oxcarts creak along the roads to homes nearby. The Water Festival is over.

But next year and the next and the next there will be other festivals, for everyone in Cambodia loves a holiday.

8

A WEDDING
IN PHNOM PENH

In Cambodia, such events as the birth of a child, a boy's entrance into the *wat* to begin training as a *bonze*, a wedding, or a funeral are the high occasions of family life and are often elaborately celebrated. Ancient rituals and customs are handed down from one generation to another and are meticulously observed. But a young man or woman who has worked for Americans, or studied abroad for a year or so, may introduce into these occasions some Western customs as well. Here is a description of the wedding of Heng Suor, a young man who grew up in the traditional ways of his ancestors but who also worked for the Cambodian Ministry of Education, studied for a year in the United States, and worked in cooperation with many Americans in the education division of the United States Operations Mission. During the ceremony he observed all the ancient rituals of his religion and of his people, but he wore Western clothes part of the time, had knives and forks as well as chopsticks at the tables for his wedding feast, and had music provided by both a Western and a Cambodian orchestra.

On the morning of the first day of Heng Suor's wedding children gathered in the street near the home of his uncle, waiting for his wedding procession.

"Here they come!" shouted little Neari to all the children of the neighborhood, who had been patiently standing in the dry, dusty street for over two hours, waiting for the wedding procession to appear. Cambodian children are like that. They will wait and stand or sit and look for hours; even the naked babies straddling the hips of most of the eight- or ten-year-old boys and girls patiently wait and look.

The black eyes of Neari and her friends shone with anticipation, but they did not crowd the marchers in the street. They were standing well back, but constantly watching.

The wedding procession was marching from the home of the groom's uncle, where many of his relatives from out of town had gathered, to the home of his bride, Sar Chantis, about four blocks away.

Neari and the children watching for the wedding procession

It was nine o'clock on Saturday, April 4, and it was already hot. Heng Suor's dignified uncle led the procession, carrying a large tray on which was balanced a bright red, cellophane-wrapped package. After him came dozens of friends and relatives, each carrying a gift wrapped in bright-colored cellophane.

"It's really a big one," Neari whispered to Hang Lai. "The friends are generous. He must have many. Oh, isn't it pretty!"

Now the procession was right in front of her. She wanted to touch that big red cellophane ball.

The children watched eagerly and called to one another.

"There are five pineapples!"

"He has onions!"

"Oh, what a big jar of cookies!"

Their mouths watered as all these gifts of food went by in their bright red, green, or pink wrappings. There were also gifts of lengths of silk, and of silver.

"Isn't it a long procession!"

"He must be very rich!"

Members of the wedding procession bearing gifts

"I'm going to run all the way and see the bride," called Neari as she shifted her heavy little brother to the other hip.

At last the end of the procession came into view. All the children rushed into the street and followed it happily, block after block, no one minding the heat or dust or flies or mosquitoes.

"That's her place! There it is, there's the bride's house, where that big canopy is."

"Yes, see his uncle leading them in!" shouted Neari.

Soon all the children were in the yard, surrounding the procession.

The front of the house, which stood on stilts about six feet above the ground, was open to the air. Inside, the children could see the elders sitting in a circle on the floor of the square room, both the men and the women dressed in black. Each gift was taken up the short steps and deposited in front of one elder, until soon the whole room was filled with the bright-colored packages. It looked as much like Christmas Eve in an American home as a Saturday morning wedding in Cambodia.

The canopy-covered yard was crowded with friends and relatives, and Neari and the other children were running everywhere. The small boys all ran around naked. The bells on the anklets of the little girls tinkled. Over in one corner of the yard was the bridegroom's dressing room, a tent of sorts put up for the two days of the wedding. Heng Suor and his mother stood at the door of the temporary dressing room and greeted everyone.

There was no sign of the bride, but everyone knew that she was in the house with her mother and her attendants.

Five musicians sauntered into the yard and arranged themselves on a low platform near the house. One man had a large, boat-shaped stringed instrument with ivory frets under the strings, on which he plunked a gay melody. Another man played a different melody on his flute. A boy with a hollow wood drum beat out a strong rhythm, getting two pitches — one by hitting the drumhead hard on the edge, the other by hitting it lightly in the center. An old man sawed away on a two-string fiddle. A boy played a small cymbal and also

Cooking in the yard

sang. He had a lot of fun singing and teasing the children nearby.

Neari eased her baby brother onto the platform beside the cymbal player. She clapped her hands softly in time to the music. Nearly fifty children stood around listening to the music and sniffing all the smells from the good food cooking in the field next door.

The children had high hopes of getting something to eat. There was plenty of activity in the temporary outdoor kitchen being set up nearby. There were ten cooks with at least ten helpers, and they all had plenty to do.

Four unwilling, squealing fat pigs were causing a big commotion as they were being prepared for cooking. Three men dug the pit and put up the pole on which the pigs were to be stretched and barbecued. Over one of eight fires that had been built in large, shallow holes, another man was boiling dozens of crabs. A fifth was popping many chickens into kettles of boiling water. Others were filling big pots with rice noodles.

A long bench at the end of the yard was spread with many kinds of vegetables: squash, tomatoes, corn, beans, water chestnuts, bean sprouts, peas, and mushrooms.

By evening a grand feast would be prepared. In the meantime the cooks and helpers were busy, but not too busy to give some rice or

The groom greets his bride

fish or crab to a hungry child or to a family just arrived for the wedding from a village up-country. All day long the cooks fed snacks to some guests and to some of the uninvited children, and prepared the huge feast for one hundred and fifty invited guests. All day long the little orchestra played and played. The children ate, slept, danced, played games, and watched.

About two o'clock in the afternoon the bridegroom came out of his small dressing room, wearing a beautiful red and gold brocade coat cut in Western style over a handsome Cambodian *sampot* of blue and gold brocade. He wore long black stockings and polished black shoes such as a Western man would wear. A hush fell over the guests. This was an important moment. He walked slowly to the house, mounted the steps, and sat down beside a long, narrow table on which were arranged offerings of fruit and flowers and burning incense sticks. In the center was a silver bowl with scissors and comb. The gay young cymbal-player from the orchestra came up the steps behind him.

Then the beautiful, petite bride appeared, dressed in a gold brocade *sampot* with a bodice of bright red silk drapery over one shoulder. She wore several golden chain necklaces over the drapery, many golden bracelets on each arm, and two heavy golden anklets with serpent heads on each ankle. A wreath of small artificial flowers rested on the black hair above her delicate face, which had been made up with great skill. She sat down beside the bridegroom. The cymbal-player then danced around the table several times, pausing to cut a bit of hair from the groom's head and a bit from the bride's head, and chanting a song about this symbolic rite of cleansing the mind by cutting the hair. Soon others joined him in a *lamthon* dance around the table. The cymbal-player sang and joked, teasing the bride and groom.

The bride and groom enjoyed the clowning, but custom demanded that they soon retire to their separate rooms. Quiet reigned for an hour. The sun shone brightly over the house, the kitchen in the field next door, the orchestra, and the children.

Before long the *achsah*, or marriage arranger, arrived. He rolled out a straw mat in front of the house and slowly and carefully set up an altar with vases of flowers, bowls of fruit, and burning incense.

About three o'clock a new hush fell over the guests. Quietly, solemnly, the groom walked out of his room again, this time wearing a blue brocade coat. He knelt on a cushion in front of the altar arranged beautifully on the ground, bowing his head and saying appropriate prayers.

Five Buddhist *bonzes* ascended the steps to the house and sat in their saffron robes against the wall behind the circle of elders. Each *bonze* was given cigarettes and a glass of cold water. The bride, still dressed in gorgeous gold brocade and golden jewelry, appeared for the second time at her door. The *achsah* knelt in front of the *bonzes*. The bride and groom knelt on red satin cushions behind him.

The *achsah* and the *bonzes* began the beautiful and solemn antiphonal chanting of a ritual hymn, tossing the melody back and forth. The orchestra played softly but steadily.

When this religious ceremony ended, the guests grew more restive than ever. The laughter was loud, and spirits ran high. But by tradition the bride and groom once more retired alone to their separate rooms. They rested for two hours until the sun began to set in a flowing copper sky. As night fell softly over the happy crowd, Neari and her friends reluctantly ate their last tidbit of crab and water chestnut, and then slowly — and oh, so sadly — left in tiny groups, exhausted but exhilarated.

Soon the caterer's helpers set up twenty round tables, each seating eight people. They placed the silver and glasses on white cloths. They hung brightly colored lanterns all about. As night fell, the air vibrated with the whirling insects attracted to the lights.

A silver urn ready to receive all the gifts of money was placed on a table near the entrance. This wedding would cost close to five thousand riels (about fourteen hundred dollars), and, like every

*Heng Suor
saying prayers
at the improvised
Buddhist altar*

Cambodian groom, Heng Suor had borrowed the money for the wedding from a bank and hoped to receive about that much from his wedding gifts. He hoped he would not be "out at the bank," as one says. Every invited guest dropped a one-hundred-, two-hundred-, or five-hundred-riel note in the large silver urn, which was graciously presided over by a close friend of the groom.

A new orchestra of ten Western wind instruments, drums, and a bass viol was set up in the living room. It played mostly Western music. Its blaring drowned out the gentle music being made by the Cambodian orchestra, which, however, still played on in the yard. The elders were already sitting at the head table. Heng Suor and his parents greeted guests, who soon filled all the tables, and the feast

The groom presents his bride to the wedding guests

was on: drink, soup, fowl, fish, soup, fowl, fish, and rice — one dish after another. The groom continued to greet friends, but still the bride was not to be seen.

Finally, when it was almost eleven o'clock and the guests were very gay, the bride appeared at her door, a handmaiden behind her bearing a large basket. The groom took her hand and led her from one table to the next. From the basket she took cigarettes wrapped in small pink or lavender hand-hemstitched kerchiefs and handed one to each guest. The groom lit each guest's cigarette, and good wishes were exchanged.

The feast was over, but both orchestras still played on. Again the bride and groom returned to their separate rooms. In the yard relatives set up cots surrounded by mosquito nets and put their families to bed. The insects hummed softly, the mosquitoes bit gently. The orchestras ceased playing and the Western orchestra left. Time passed. The night was dark.

The chief astrologer had studied long and carefully, reading the horoscopes of both the bridegroom and the bride, and of both their

124   CAMBODIA

parents. He had calculated the relative positions of the sun, moon, and stars, observed the direction of the wind, and set the hour for the tying ceremony at 3 A.M. As the early morning hour approached, a few close friends and family began to gather. Some guests got up from their outdoor beds. Some slept on, snoring gently. The night was dark.

Then, exactly at three, in the still blue-black hour before dawn, the groom came out of his tent in still another outfit — a mauve-colored knee-length cloak of sheer chiffon, heavily embroidered in silk and beads. With slow, dignified pace he crossed the yard and mounted the steps to the living room, passing the out-of-town visitors in all stages of dress.

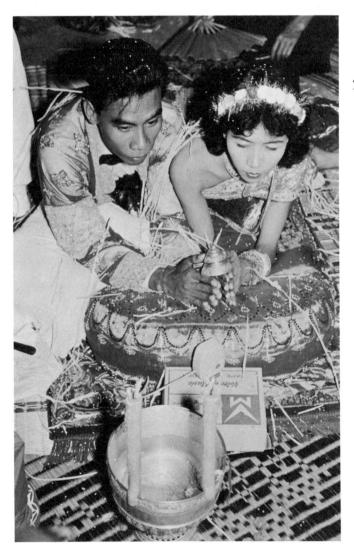

The tying ceremony

The bride appeared at her door in a new brocade, the loveliest of all, still wearing her gorgeous golden jewelry. Most of the clothes and jewelry of both the bride and bridegroom had been rented for the occasion, as is the custom.

The *achsah* had set up an altar in the center of the room, in the midst of the elders. Long green satin pillows were at one side. The bride and groom each half knelt, half lay down on these pillows with their right arms stretched out in front. The *achsah* led a chant. Soon he lit a candle which was passed around the circle of elders thirteen times. Each elder passed his hand over the flame as it went around, thus assuring that no evil spirits could influence this marriage. The *achsah* tied the bride's and groom's hands together with a long red silk thread. The elders and guests had prepared themselves with handfuls of the tiny seeds from the center of long palm flowers. As the ceremony ended, they threw these over the bride and groom, much as guests at a wedding in the Western world throw rice.

The little bride broke her hand free of the thread and fled to her room. The bridegroom could not enter, but he caught the tail of his bride's dress and gave it a flip as she escaped for the last time.

It was almost five o'clock and the faint streaks of dawn began to appear as most of the guests finally left the bride's place. Phnom Penh guests were wearily going home. Some out-of-town guests were dressed, others were half dressed, others still slept. A few children began to run around. The cooks and helpers cleaned up the large outdoor kitchen. The orchestra played on, and the insects hummed until the dawn.

After a few hours of rest, the bride and groom came out to receive detailed advice about married life from the elders. A tooth-cleansing ceremony was also held to impress upon them that they should always speak well of others in their village.

Off and on all that long, hot Sunday the bride and bridegroom continued to visit courteously, joke, talk, and laugh with out-of-town family members and with friends who were still around. At last, near midnight of this second day of the ceremony, the chief elder put the couple in the marital chamber. The elders sat outside discussing the reasons why this would be a happy and successful marriage if all their instructions were obeyed.

As the gray streaks of Monday's dawn appeared in the eastern sky, the consummation ceremony was almost over. The married couple came out hand-in-hand to receive the good wishes and blessings of the elders.

So came the second dawn.

In this wedding ceremony were rituals centuries old and customs handed down for generations side-by-side with modern ways and modern customs.

Here was music new and old.

Here were clothes of ancient design and others of modern cut.

Here was food prepared in the ways of ancestors and some in the way of modern restaurants.

Here was rigid formality and casual informality.

So the Heng Suors began their life together in the city of Phnom Penh, Cambodia.

9

PEOPLE ARE IMPORTANT

While the location of a country and the nature of its land and water may determine much of what a country is like, the most important aspect of any nation is its people. And the most important factor in any nation's future is its children.

Years ago, an American poet, Sara Teasdale, wrote two lines about children that many people love:

> Children's faces looking up
> Holding wonder like a cup.

These lines could describe a group of Cambodian children as well as a group of Western children. In Cambodia, little children feel loved and wanted. Almost every child is carried on the hip of an older brother or sister until he is two or three years old, so that even as an infant he takes part in his family's work and play. Little boys are seen with their fathers at work, little girls with their mothers. The family, like the village, is a closely knit group. The children share in all that goes on. They look happy and interested in the life around them — and they truly are.

An increasing number of Cambodian children are going to the government and pagoda schools as more and more people see the need for education. The people who live in the provinces want

Children's faces

their children to be educated as much as do those who live in the cities of Battambang, Kompong Cham, and Phnom Penh.

Most of the schools are lower schools, and after a student has finished these lower schools he may continue his studies with a tutor. Some Chinese students go to "Practical English Colleges," of which there are twenty or more in Phnom Penh, to learn English, so that they can go on to school in the United States or Europe. Even if they do not plan to go abroad, many students are eager to learn to speak English, which they recognize as the language of international communication. Many wish to become doctors or engineers. Some go on to study in the government lycée schools in the big cities. But so far relatively few of the total Cambodian population go beyond the third grade.

One excellent contribution of the United States' foreign-aid program is the well-equipped English-teaching language laboratory in Phnom Penh. The government selects ten or twelve Cambodians each year to study with a linguist in this laboratory and learn

Orchestra playing for the opening ceremonies at Kompong Kantuot

English well enough to teach it in a Cambodian secondary school. In addition, a small Khmer-American school, consisting so far of only four grades, is being set up with American aid and counsel. Both its curriculum and its teaching techniques are similar to those of an American elementary school. The teachers have been trained in the United States. English instead of French is taught in the fourth grade. Many are watching this experiment with great interest.

Another fine and growing institution developed with American funds is the Rural Teacher Training College in Kompong Kantuot. In 1956 nine hundred young men and women who had completed the sixth grade took competitive examinations to enter this school. Seventy-five boys and seventy-five girls were accepted and began their teacher training under a Cambodian staff counseled and directed by a carefully selected group of American educators. That first class graduated in June 1961. Each year between three hundred and four hundred new students are admitted. The entrance of several hundred well-trained teachers into the schools of the country each year will improve the quality of Cambodian education as it moves from traditional rote training to more modern methods. Not only are basic language skills, mathematics, and good manners being taught, but also world geography, history, modern science, and languages, especially English. Each student of Kompong Kantuot is pledged to teach in government schools for at least ten years after his graduation. Ho Tung Ho ably directs this college, which will have a significant influence upon Cambodian education.

Special summer workshops teaching new concepts of health, of teaching, of psychology, and of child development are held in the capital each year. All are helping to improve the quality of instruction in the schools.

The children of tomorrow in Cambodia will need books like those American children now have. They will be eager to know what people in the United States are like and will want to study and work with them. Some of them will study in America, the Philippines, France and other countries. Several thousand Cambodian students do this each year. They can learn many things from us, but they can also teach us much that we need to learn. Their spiritual values, sense of time, sense of humor, patience, kindliness, as well as some of their manual and artistic skills would be very valuable to us.

In Phnom Penh you may see fine groups of young men, dressed in Western clothes. Many of these are students from the lycée or workers in foreign offices. Some have been working for Americans under our foreign-aid program and are going to the Philippines for further training in technical education. They are called "participants" by the Americans — participants in an exchange program of training young people to grow better rice, to know more about health and education, and so to strengthen Cambodia. These comprise one of the most important groups of young people in Cambodia today.

But the vast majority of Cambodian people still live their lives with little or no schooling. These are the vendors, the rice growers, the fishermen of traditional Cambodia. You see interesting people such as these gathered at any market: an old man exhibits real wit as he bargains for a good price; two fishermen who know how to sell fish as well as to catch; the vegetable boys, balancing their long poles over their shoulders with heavy baskets at either end.

How straight and poised are the women with baskets on their heads, carrying produce to market and good food home! They begin as very little girls by carrying small baskets of fruit or sugar cane. The grace, and skill, and erect posture of the women, who can often balance two or more baskets on their heads at once, are beautiful to see.

There are not many beggars in Cambodia, but there is a very picturesque one who has been around the market for a long time. He has very long fingernails, and he reminds one of a Chinese mandarin who does not need to work. This old musician has made himself into a character who attracts attention.

Then there are the *bonzes*. Day after day, before eleven o'clock in the morning, one sees them along the streets, stopping in front of homes and waiting with their food bowls. The younger ones go to class after eating; the older ones, to the temples to meditate and pray or to pagoda schools to teach.

Almost all Cambodians like to sing and dance. In a village up-country, the drummer gathers most of the inhabitants around a fire and leads them in singing the well-known ancient Khmer songs and in dancing the beautiful *lamthon*. The Asia Foundation gave Meng Mao, director of the Bureau of Technical Services of the Cambodian Ministry of Education, recording equipment. He has gone into many villages to record this ancient folk music.

If you went with Meng Mao to a workers' village near Paillin across from the government rubber plantation, you would see little Chum Tith. He is almost nine years old. The sun is setting, and all the children have had their evening rice. Chum Tith wanders across the fields, singing and clapping his hands. He stops near a stone and faces the other children. His dark eyes are shining. He lifts up his face and starts a gay song, leading the whole group with his arms,

*Participants ready
to leave for study
in the Philippines*

*A little girl
selling sugar cane*

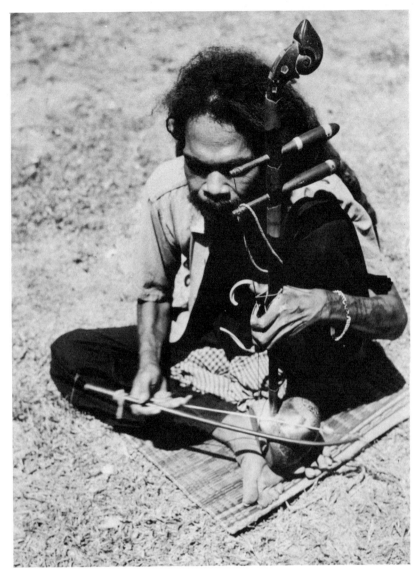

Cambodia's most picturesque beggar

his entire body moving in rhythm. Then he changes the song as well as the mood and rhythm. The other children follow his lead and sing and sing. As the sun disappears and the stars begin to fill the dark sky, Mao Man, the village drummer, comes down to join the children. At first he drums softly with Chum Tith, then louder and louder. With the next song he takes over the leadership. After a few more songs, the children follow Mao Man back across the fields to the village, where some of the boys have built a small fire in the open space in the center of it.

Mao Man takes his place at one side; the children settle down in a wide circle around the fire. All the villagers come out and join them. Mao Man begins to sing to his drumming accompaniment. The people join in. He changes to another rhythm and urges the villagers to dance — first one couple, then another. The men take their places behind the women and move in a circle around the fire. Their arms and hands and fingers move in the slow rhythmic beauty of the *lamthon* dance's age-old patterns. They sing several songs; all the older people sing too. Songs and dances, dances and songs handed down from their Khmer forebears fill the still tropic night, this night and many others — in Paillin and in many villages like this one.

Meng Mao and a group of young people in Phnom Penh broadcast a program of Cambodian songs for half an hour every afternoon. The group sings at home and at school and is now helping to prepare an expanded program of music for broadcast as more and more Cambodians obtain radios.

The men who head Cambodia's Ministries of Health, Education, Agriculture, Foreign Affairs, Information, Affairs of State, and Law are the leaders of the nation today. Most of them were educated in France or at some university outside Cambodia. They speak French, for it is the official language of the state, although many are learning English. Nick Tioulong, Plek Chat, Sorn Saun, Phy Ten Lai, and Yem Yissim are among the men in this leadership group.

But the real leader of Cambodia is her popular prince, Norodom Sihanouk. Sihanouk had been king of Cambodia for some years under French rule, but in 1954 he abdicated in order to be free from the constitutional and cultural restrictions which prohibited royalty from participating in politics. He turned the kingship back to his father and became the premier instead. Now as a practical politician he is building the most efficient political organization Cambodia has ever known. He uses the newspapers, the radio, the Royal Palace grounds for getting his hopes and plans across to the people. His party is known as Sangkum Reastr Niyum, the People's Socialist Community. There is a rival group, the Democratic party, led by a former nationalist rebel who is said to have pro-communist connections. There are three or four small regional parties also, but the people love their prince and like his many good ideas, so the Sangkum holds the political power.

Prince Norodom Sihanouk

After the death of his father in 1960, Sihanouk resigned as premier, with the recommendation that his successor be selected by the people from the ministers of his former government. But the people wanted their prince to head the government, so in June of that year Sihanouk agreed to become chief of state, a new post that still has rather undefined powers.

Sihanouk is pledged to a policy of political neutrality.

At the Belgrade Conference of nonaligned nations, Prince Sihanouk said, "I believe that both blocs (Western and Communist) should understand that certain countries are capable of giving them disinterested aid, which they may use or not. These countries have no material power, but they have one precious thing, which is their good will and good faith."

He also said, "While waiting patiently for a disarmament agreement among the great powers, we hope, along with the great majority of the peoples of the world, that the 'atomic' nations will consent to halt again, and at once, their dangerous experiments."

Prince Sihanouk is an attractive man with bright, intelligent brown eyes under heavy black brows. He is alert and sensitive, with an air of easy authority. He loves music, plays a saxophone in his own band, and composes music. He is most widely acclaimed for his "Miniature Suite" based upon Cambodian folk tunes. The Air Force Symphony Orchestra in Washington, as well as other American orchestras, has performed it.

The prince's main job is to build a strong central government for and of his own people, a government able to resist the strong and conflicting external forces around his land. Cambodia's strategic position in the future of Southeast Asia is evident. This small nation, where the ancient and the modern are in juxtaposition, must find a way of adjusting to the changing world.

It is as if one arm is holding onto the past while the other stretches out to take hold of the future.

Prince Sihanouk and his people are training themselves to make critical decisions these days concerning the following problems, as well as many more:

1. HEALTH. What is good health for the Cambodian? Should his life expectancy be as long as that of people of the Western world? Cambodia's standards of sanitation and cleanliness are, like most of these in other Oriental countries, very different from those of the West. Should they be changed? Religious taboos and customs affect many patterns of behavior, and new practices are often very difficult to introduce. For example, a Buddhist will not kill even flies and

Should he be educated?

*What about school
for this little country girl?*

mosquitoes, which spread malaria, dysentery and other diseases. Ways of fighting disease and of raising the standard of living have to be worked out slowly, in terms of Cambodian culture, the Buddhist religion, and the physical conditions in this tropic land. But everywhere in Cambodia today one sees cleaner children, cleaner

Will this young merchant of Phnom Penh need regular studies?

schools, cleaner wells in villages. And one sees more children and adults in better clinics. So there are many encouraging signs of changes that will build a healthier people.

2. EDUCATION. Should every child be educated? This new idea is spreading rapidly throughout the country. About 350,000 children are now in government and pagoda schools, and the number is increasing. Teachers are getting better training. But as more and more young people obtain higher education, more and more jobs that can use their increased abilities, skills, and training will have to be developed. Better schools, better teachers, and more books and equipment will develop a people better able to help Cambodia take its place in the modern family of nations.

3. GOVERNMENT. Can a constitutional monarchy in a country where most people do not read gain enough stability to hold its own as a nonaligned nation, particularly in the strategic situation in which Cambodia finds itself? Cambodia has come a long way with its colorful limited elections and the attempts made by the government to explain its politics to the people. This nation needs trained leaders with courage, insight, and wisdom. Prince Sihanouk and his ministers face a grave challenge as they seek to find the means for a secure and continuing happy life for the people of Cambodia.

This ancient land of the Khmers — with its proud cultural heritage, its love of beauty expressed in music, dance, and other arts, its strong allegiance to the Buddhist faith, its determination to educate its people for the world as it is today, and its resolve to maintain its political neutrality in the power struggle of East and West — is a land of contrasts, a land of challenge. Here is Cambodia, a nation slowly emerging from the cocoon of its ancient ways, not quite sure of the shape and colors of its unfolding wings.

INDEX

Numbers in italics refer to illustrations.

DATE DUE

GAYLORD			PRINTED IN U.S.A.